the egg cookbook

Exceptionally delicious recipes for eggs any time of the day

pil

Publications International, Ltd

Pictured on the front cover: Vegetable Quinoa Frittata *(page 34)*.

Pictured on the back cover *(clockwise from top left):* Crustless Spinach Quiche *(page 25)*, Scotch Eggs *(page 88)* and Greek Isles Omelet *(page 5)*.

ISBN: 978-1-64558-232-8

Manufactured in China.

8 7 6 5 4 3 2 1

Let's get social!

@Publications_International

@PublicationsInternational

www.pilbooks.com

contents

mediterranean
artichoke omelet
(page 14)

cauliflower
picnic salad
(page 82)

cheese blintzes
(page 116)

omelets & scrambles

greek isles omelet
makes 2 servings

2 tablespoons olive oil, divided

¼ cup chopped onion

¼ cup canned artichoke hearts, rinsed, drained and sliced

¼ cup chopped fresh spinach

¼ cup chopped plum tomato

2 tablespoons sliced pitted black olives, rinsed and drained

4 eggs

½ teaspoon salt

Dash black pepper

1 Heat 1 tablespoon oil in small nonstick skillet over medium heat. Add onion; cook and stir 2 minutes or until crisp-tender. Add artichokes; cook and stir until heated through. Gently stir in spinach, tomato and olives; cook 1 minute. Remove to small bowl. Wipe out skillet with paper towels.

2 Whisk eggs, salt and pepper in medium bowl until well blended.

3 Add remaining 1 tablespoon oil to skillet; heat over medium heat. Pour egg mixture into skillet; cook and stir gently, lifting edges to allow uncooked portion to flow underneath. Cook just until set.

4 Spoon vegetable mixture over half of omelet; gently loosen omelet with spatula and fold in half. Cut in half; serve immediately.

scrambled eggs with smoked salmon

makes 4 servings

8 eggs
⅛ teaspoon salt
⅛ teaspoon black pepper
1 tablespoon butter
2 tablespoons sliced green onions
1 ounce cold cream cheese, cut into ¼-inch cubes
2 ounces smoked salmon, flaked

1 Whisk eggs, salt and pepper in large bowl until well blended.

2 Melt butter in medium nonstick skillet over medium heat. Pour egg mixture into skillet; cook 5 to 7 minutes or until eggs begins to set, stirring occasionally and scraping bottom of pan.

3 Gently fold in green onions, cream cheese and salmon; cook and stir about 3 minutes or just until eggs are cooked through but still slightly moist.

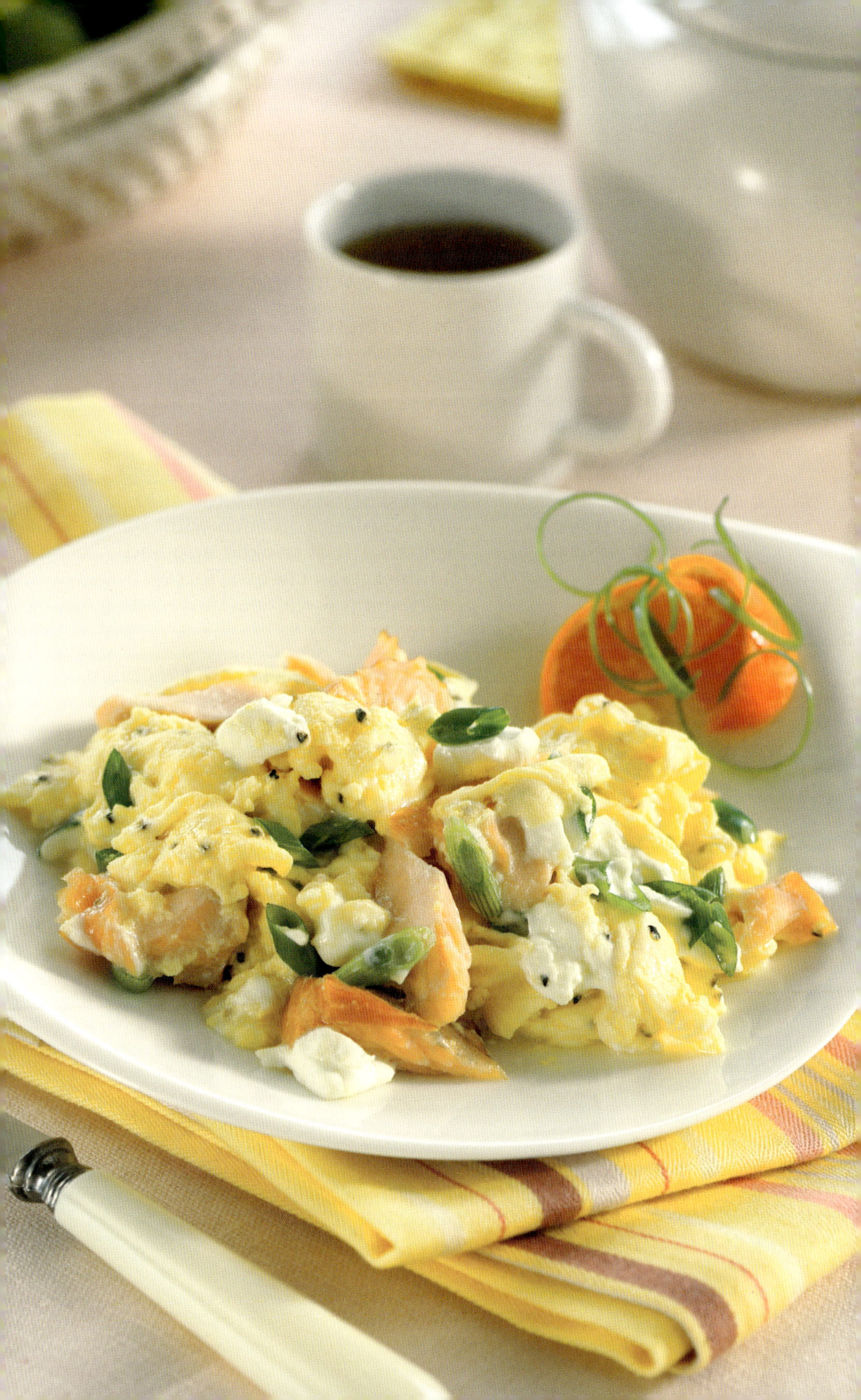

ham and egg mini wafflewiches

makes 2 servings (2 wafflewiches each)

2 eggs
  Salt and black
    pepper
6 teaspoons butter,
    divided
8 frozen mini waffles
2 thin slices deli ham
    (about 1 ounce
    each), cut in half
4 tablespoons
    (1 ounce) shredded
    Cheddar cheese

1 Whisk eggs, salt and pepper in small bowl until well blended.

2 Melt 2 teaspoons butter in small nonstick skillet over medium heat. Pour egg mixture into skillet; cook and stir just until set.

3 Spread one side of each waffle with 1 teaspoon butter. Place ham slice on unbuttered side of 4 waffles; top each with one fourth of cooked egg and 1 tablespoon cheese. Top with remaining 4 waffles, buttered side up.

4 Heat medium skillet over medium heat. Cook sandwiches 4 minutes per side or until cheese melts and waffles are golden brown, pressing down with back of spatula.

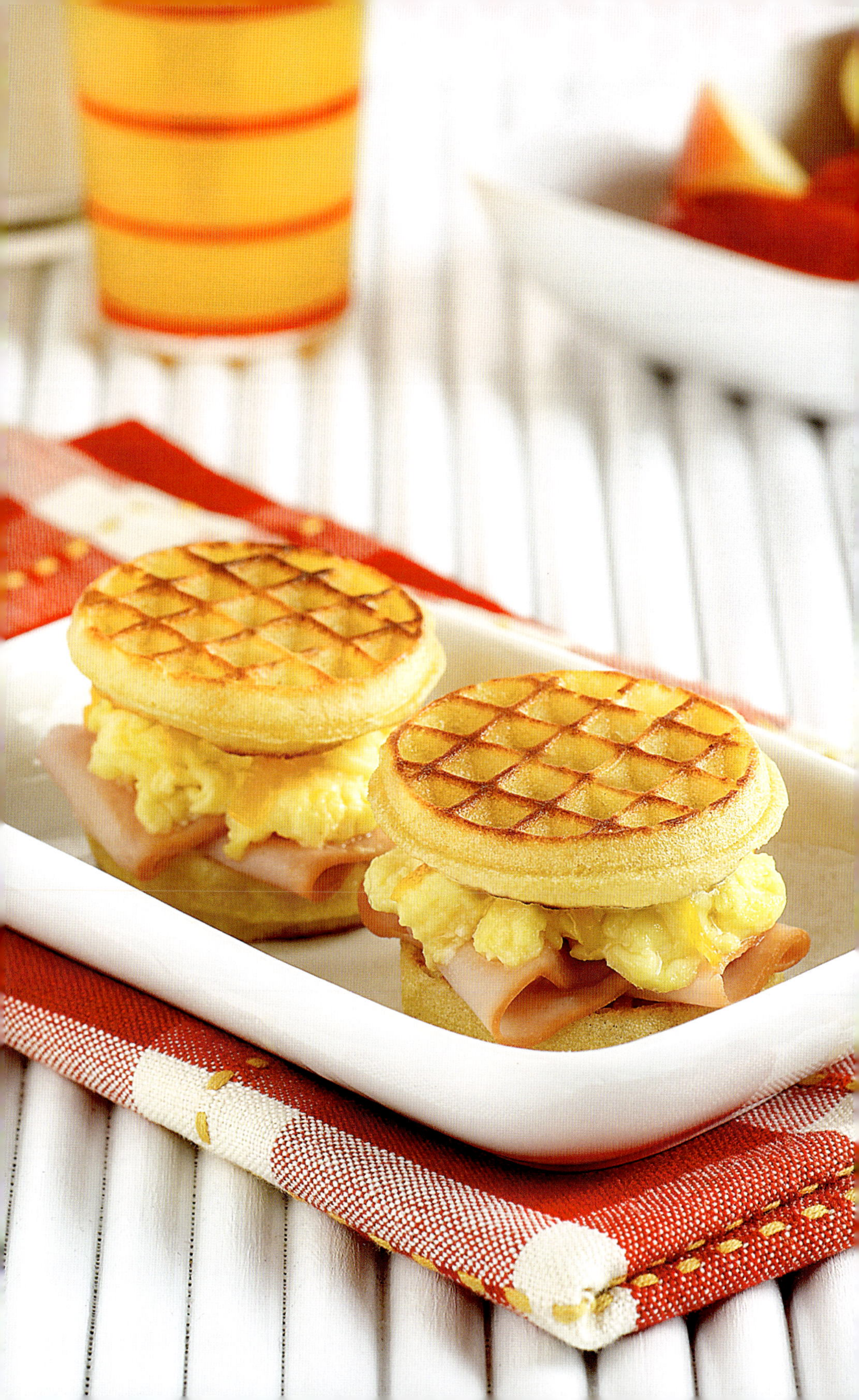

zucchini omelet with dill

makes 2 servings

4 eggs

2 tablespoons milk

½ teaspoon dried dill weed

¼ teaspoon salt

⅛ teaspoon black pepper

2 teaspoons butter

1 cup diced zucchini

1 Whisk eggs, milk, dill, salt and pepper in medium bowl until well blended.

2 Melt butter in medium nonstick skillet over medium-high heat. Add zucchini; cook 4 minutes or until lightly browned, stirring occasionally. Add egg mixture; cook until edges are set. Push edges toward center with spatula, tilting pan to allow uncooked portion to flow underneath.

3 When eggs are set, fold omelet over and cut in half.

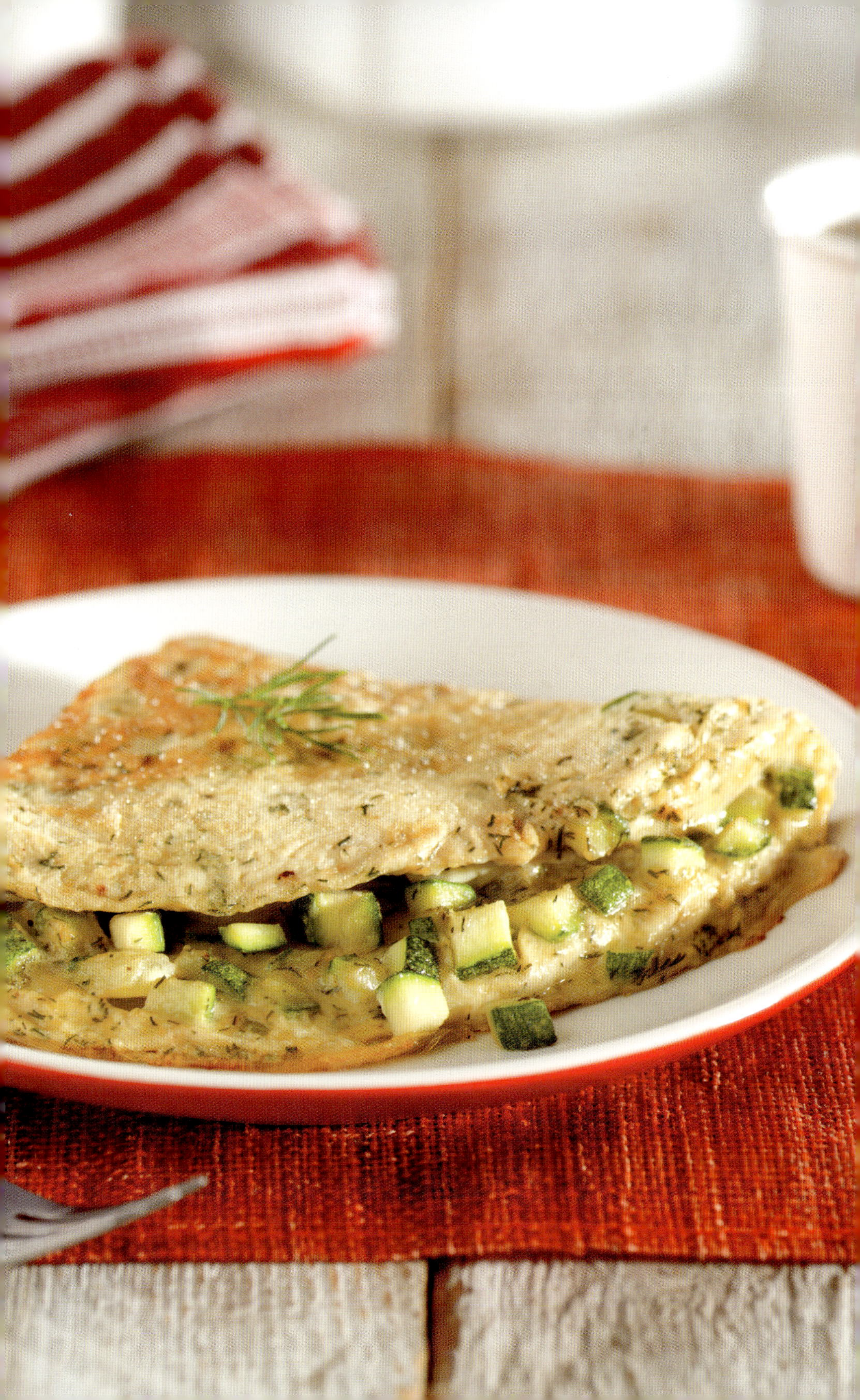

scrambled egg pile-ups

makes 1 serving

2 eggs
2 tablespoons milk
   Salt and black
      pepper
¼ cup diced orange or
      red bell pepper
1 green onion, thinly
      sliced
¼ cup grape tomatoes,
      quartered (about
      6 tomatoes)
¼ cup (1 ounce)
      shredded Cheddar
      cheese
   Sour cream
      (optional)

1 Preheat waffle maker to medium;
   spray with nonstick cooking spray.

2 Whisk eggs, milk, salt and black
   pepper in small bowl until well
   blended.

3 Working quickly, pour egg
   mixture onto waffle maker;
   sprinkle with bell pepper, green
   onion and tomatoes. Close and
   cook 2 minutes or until puffed.

4 Remove "waffle" to plate; sprinkle
   with cheese. Top with sour cream,
   if desired. Serve immediately.

tip

To remove from the waffle maker,
place a plate over the egg and flip
the egg onto the plate. Or, use the
tip of a fork to gently release the
egg from the waffle maker, then
slide a wide spatula underneath
to gently remove the egg.

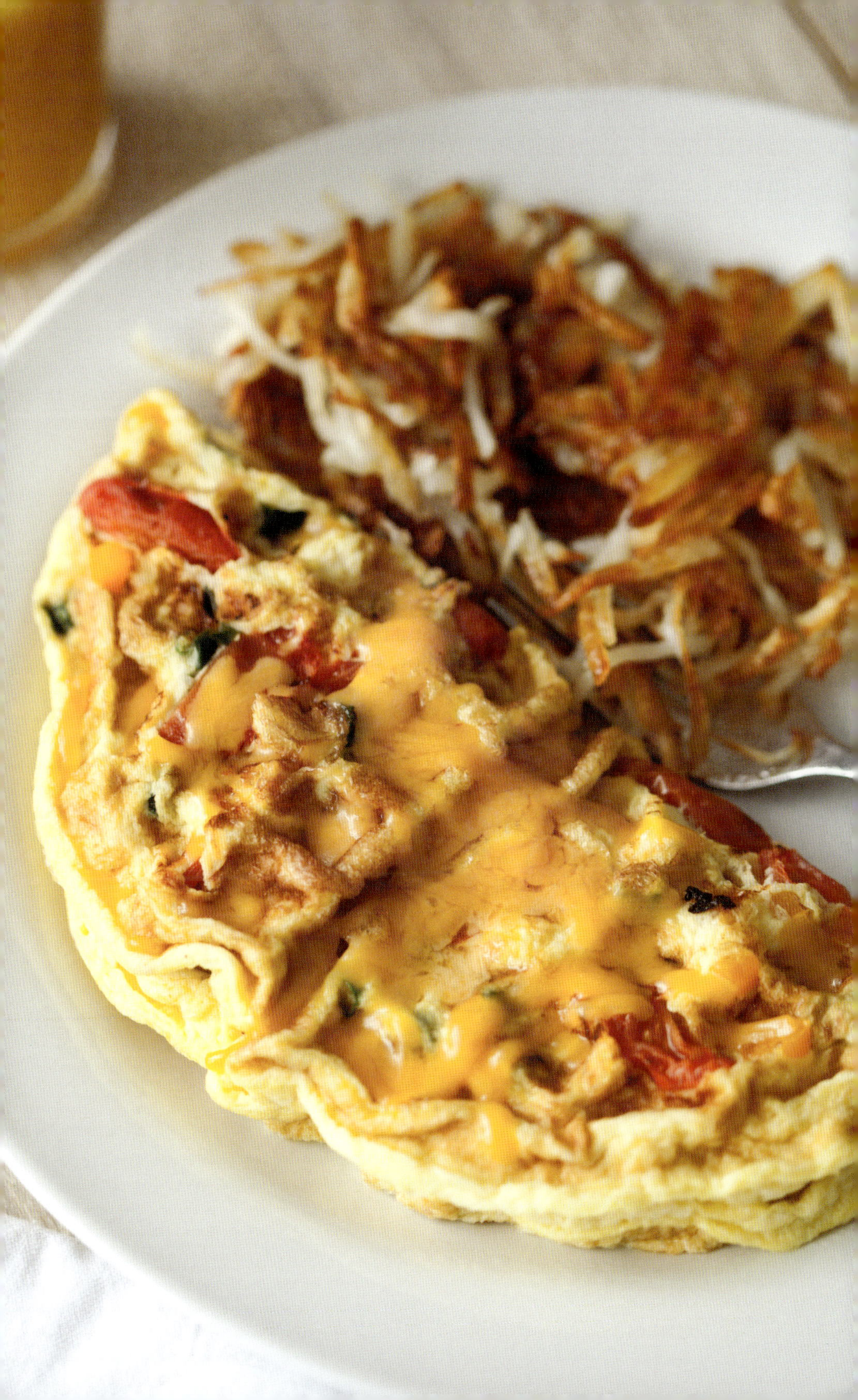

mediterranean artichoke omelet

makes 1 serving

2 eggs

1 tablespoon grated Parmesan cheese

2 tablespoons olive oil

3 cans (14 ounces each) artichoke bottoms packed in water, drained and diced

1 ounce (about 2 pieces) roasted red peppers, diced

½ teaspoon minced garlic

2 tablespoons tomato salsa

1 Whisk eggs and cheese in small bowl until well blended.

2 Heat oil in large skillet over medium-high heat. Add artichokes; cook and stir 2 to 3 minutes or until beginning to brown. Add roasted peppers; cook and stir 2 minutes or until liquid has evaporated. Add garlic; cook and stir 30 seconds. Remove to small plate; keep warm.

3 Add egg mixture to skillet; cook 1 to 2 minutes or until almost set, lifting edges with spatula to allow uncooked portion to flow underneath.

4 Spoon artichoke mixture onto half of omelet; fold omelet over filling. Cook 2 minutes or until set. Serve with salsa.

note

Raw eggs will turn green if combined with raw artichokes because of a chemical reaction between the two foods. Cooking the artichokes separately will prevent this from happening.

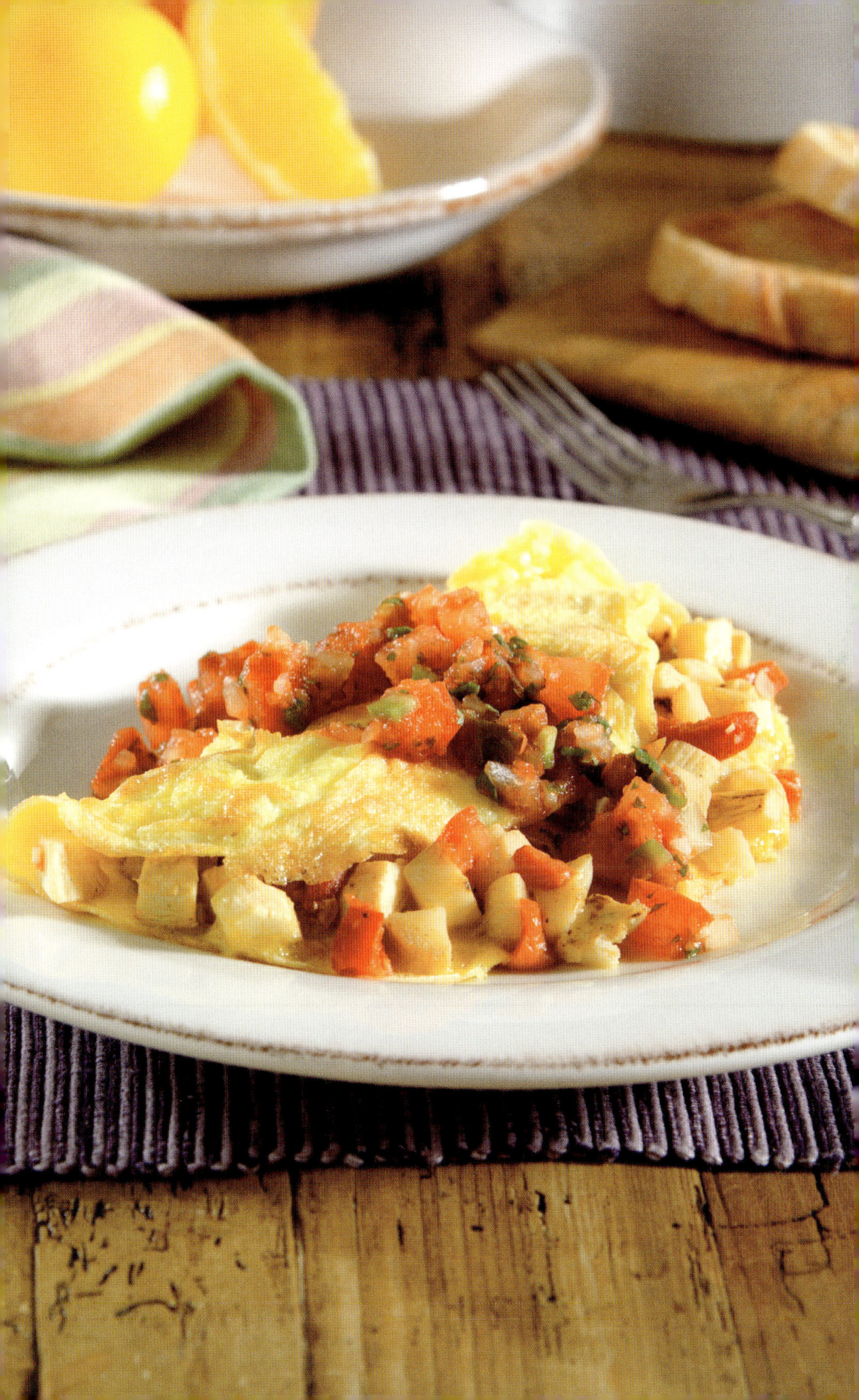

denver scramble in hash brown cups

makes 6 servings (12 hash brown cups)

3 tablespoons butter, divided

1 package (20 ounces) refrigerated hash brown potatoes

1½ teaspoons salt, divided

6 eggs

2 tablespoons milk

⅛ teaspoon black pepper

⅛ teaspoon hot pepper sauce or to taste

½ cup diced onion (¼-inch pieces)

½ cup diced green bell pepper (¼-inch pieces)

½ cup diced ham (¼-inch pieces)

⅓ cup shredded Monterey Jack cheese

1 Preheat oven to 400°F. Spray 12 standard (2½-inch) muffin cups with nonstick cooking spray.

2 Melt 2 tablespoons butter. Combine melted butter, potatoes and 1 teaspoon salt in large bowl; toss to coat. Press potatoes into bottoms and up sides of prepared cups (about 5 to 6 tablespoons per cup).

3 Bake about 35 minutes or until bottoms and sides are golden brown. (Insides of cups will not brown.)

4 When hash brown cups have baked 15 minutes, whisk eggs, milk, remaining ½ teaspoon salt, black pepper and hot pepper sauce in medium bowl until well blended. Melt remaining 1 tablespoon butter in large nonstick skillet over medium-high heat. Add onion; cook and stir about 3 minutes or until softened. Add bell pepper; cook and stir 4 minutes. Add ham; cook and stir 5 minutes or until bell pepper is crisp-tender. Pour egg mixture into skillet; cook 20 to to 30 seconds without stirring or just until edges begin to set. Stir around edges and across bottom of skillet with heatproof spatula, forming large curds. Cook 3 to 4 minutes or until eggs are fluffy and barely set, stirring gently.

5 Remove hash brown cups from pan. Fill with scrambled egg mixture (about ¼ cup egg mixture per cup); sprinkle with cheese.

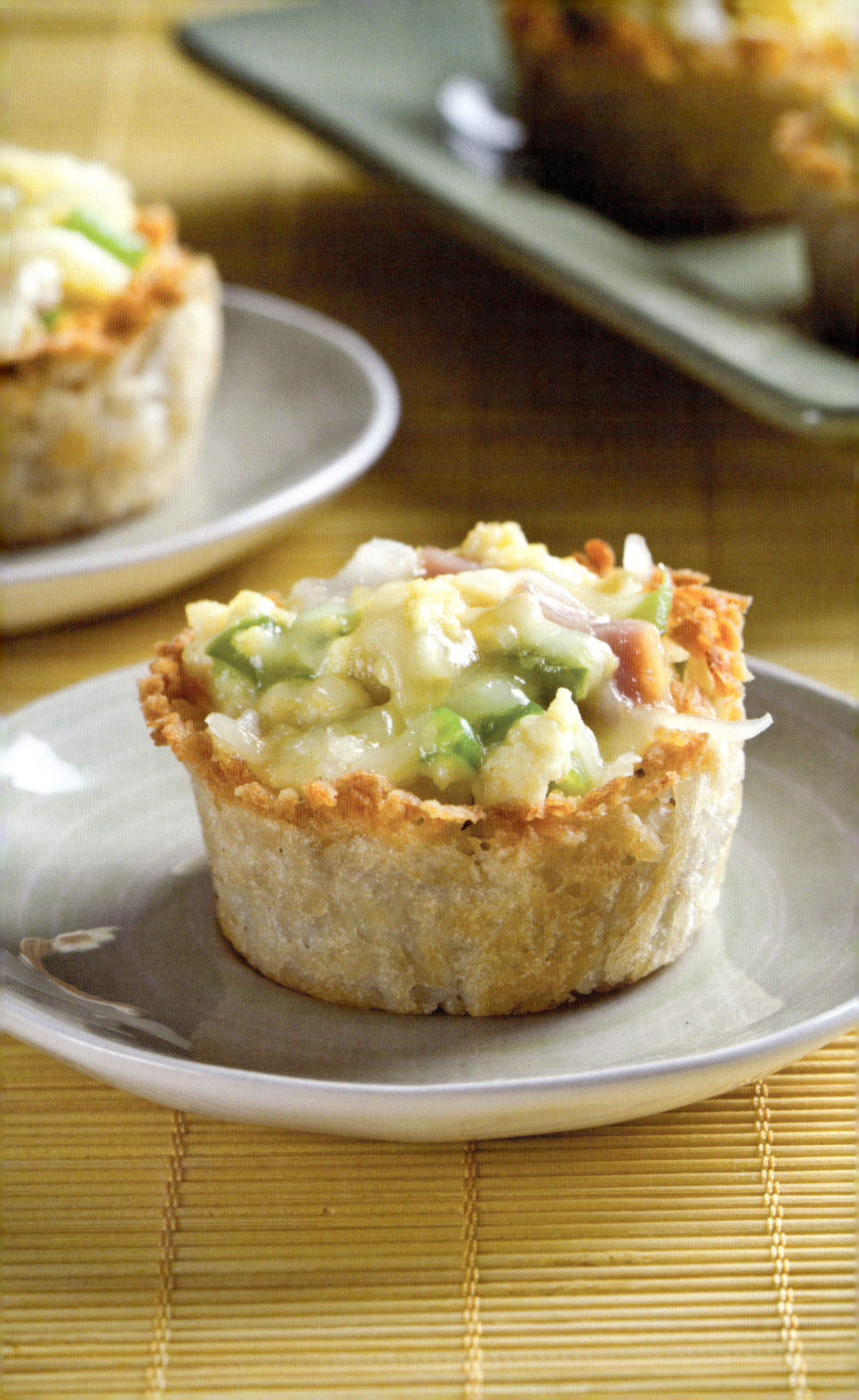

smoked salmon omelet

makes 1 serving

3 eggs

2 tablespoons milk

1 tablespoon grated Parmesan cheese

Pinch white or black pepper

1 teaspoon butter

2 tablespoons finely chopped red onion, divided

1 ounce smoked salmon, cut into 1- to 2-inch pieces

2 tablespoons sour cream

1 tablespoon water

1 tablespoon capers, rinsed and drained

Finely chopped fresh parsley (optional)

1 Whisk eggs, milk, cheese and pepper in small bowl until well blended.

2 Heat butter in small (6-inch) nonstick skillet over medium-high heat. Pour egg mixture into skillet; stir briefly. Let eggs begin to set at edges, then lift edges and tilt skillet, allowing uncooked portion of egg mixture to flow underneath. Cook about 1 minute or until omelet begins to set. Sprinkle 1 tablespoon onion over half of omelet; top with smoked salmon. Fold other half of omelet over filling; cook about 1 minute. Slide omelet onto serving plate.

3 Whisk sour cream and water in small bowl until blended. Drizzle over omelet; top with remaining 1 tablespoon onion, capers and parsley, if desired.

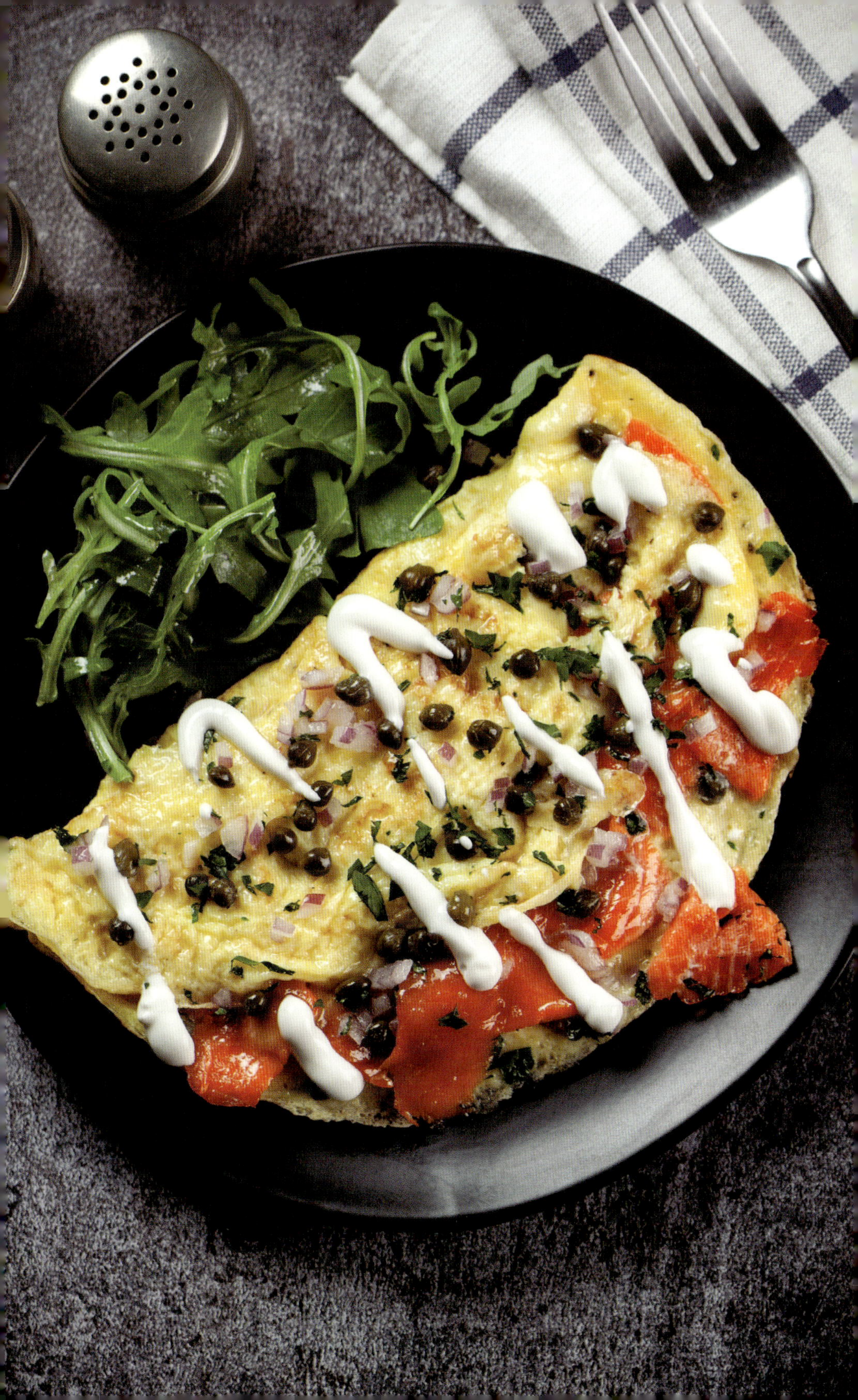

scrambled egg and red pepper pockets

makes 1 serving

2 eggs

1 tablespoon milk

⅛ teaspoon salt

⅛ teaspoon black pepper

1 tablespoon butter, softened, divided

3 tablespoons minced red onion

2 tablespoons diced jarred roasted red pepper (blot before dicing)

1 whole wheat pita bread round, cut in half crosswise

1 Whisk eggs, milk, salt and black pepper in small bowl until well blended.

2 Melt 2 teaspoons butter in medium nonstick skillet over medium heat. Add onion; cook and stir 3 to 5 minutes or until lightly browned.

3 Pour egg mixture into skillet; sprinkle with roasted peppers. Stir gently, lifting edges to allow uncooked portion to flow underneath. Cook just until set.

4 Spread inside of each pita half with remaining 1 teaspoon butter. Spoon egg mixture into pita halves.

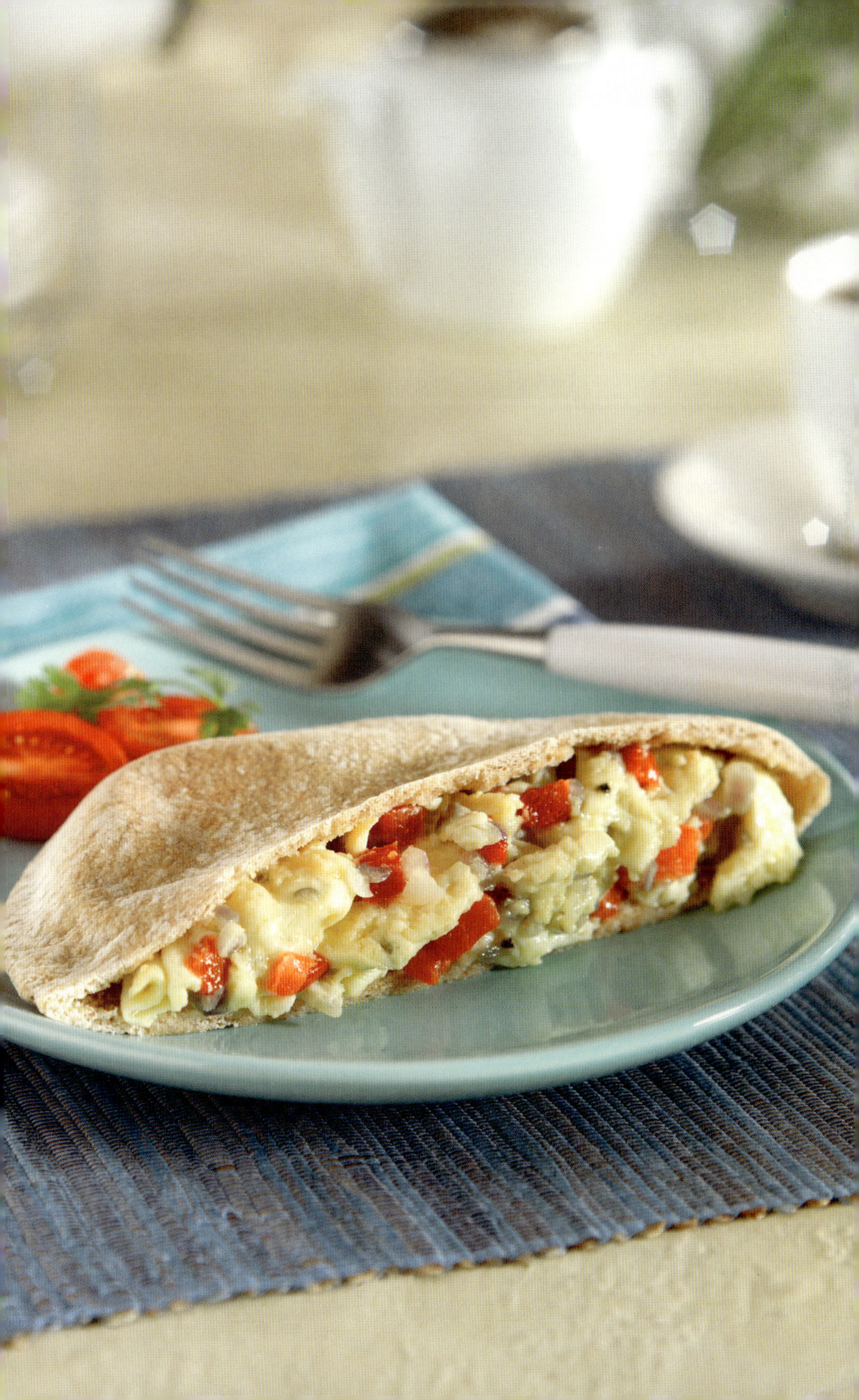

ham and vegetable omelet

makes 4 servings

1 tablespoon olive oil

2 ounces diced ham (about ½ cup)

1 small onion, diced

½ medium green bell pepper, diced

½ medium red bell pepper, diced

2 cloves garlic, minced

6 eggs, beaten

½ teaspoon salt

⅛ teaspoon black pepper

1 tablespoon butter

½ cup (2 ounces) shredded Colby cheese, divided

1 medium tomato, chopped

Hot pepper sauce (optional)

1 Heat oil in large nonstick skillet over medium-high heat. Add ham, onion, bell peppers and garlic; cook and stir 5 minutes or until vegetables are crisp-tender. Transfer to large bowl. Wipe out skillet with paper towels.

2 Whisk eggs, salt and black pepper in medium bowl until well blended.

3 Melt butter in same skillet over medium-high heat. Pour egg mixture into skillet; cook 2 minutes or until bottom is set, lifting edges with spatula to allow uncooked portion to flow underneath. Reduce heat to medium-low; cover and cook 4 minutes or until top is set.

4 Gently slide omelet onto large serving plate; spoon ham mixture down center. Sprinkle with ¼ cup cheese. Carefully fold two sides of omelet over ham mixture; sprinkle with remaining ¼ cup cheese and tomato. Cut into four wedges; serve immediately with hot pepper sauce, if desired.

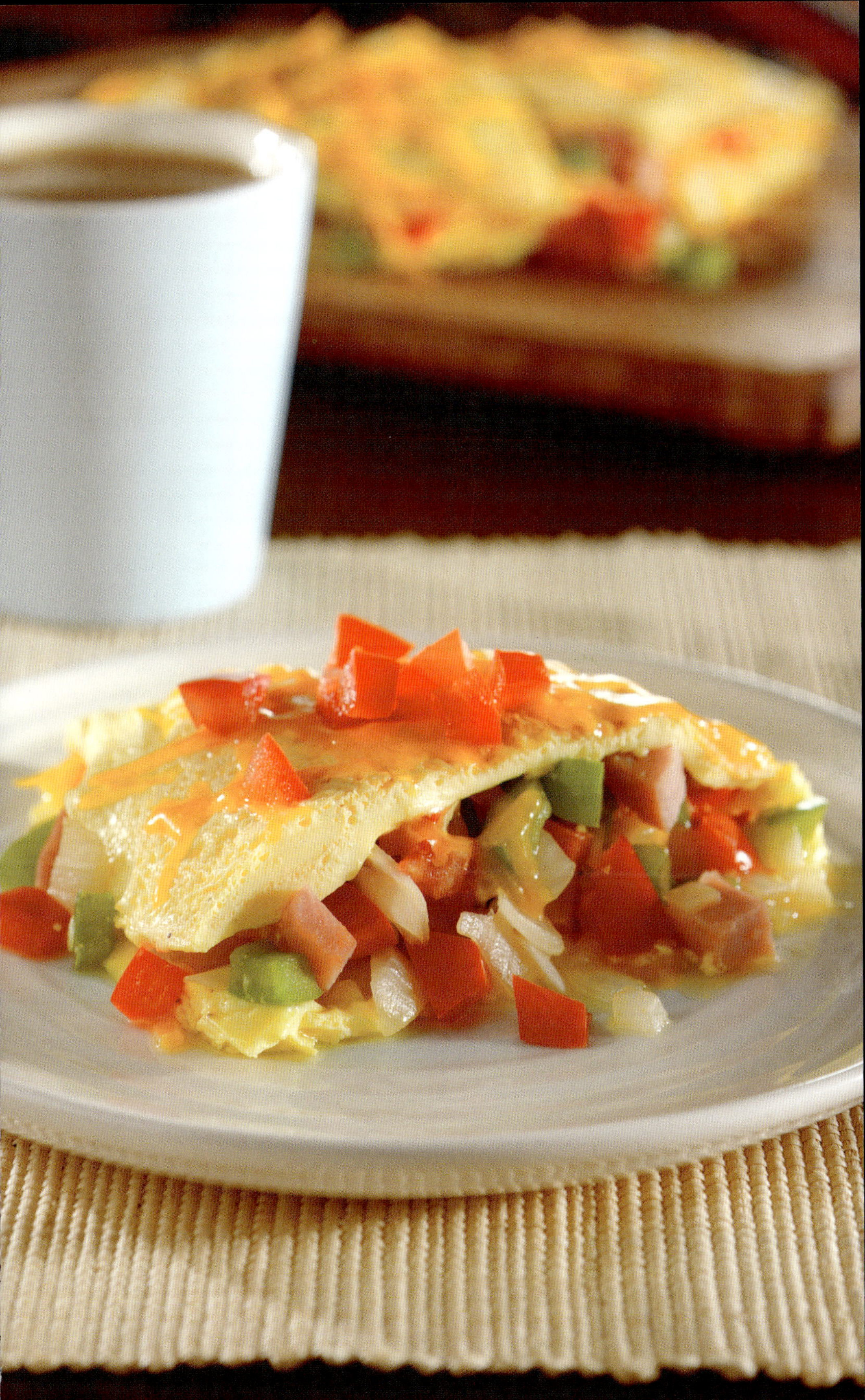

quiches & frittatas

crustless spinach quiche
makes 6 servings

8 eggs

1 cup half-and-half

1 teaspoon Italian seasoning

¾ teaspoon salt

½ teaspoon black pepper

1 package (10 ounces) frozen chopped spinach, thawed and squeezed dry

1¼ cups (5 ounces) shredded Italian cheese blend

1 Preheat oven to 350°F. Spray 8-inch round cake pan with nonstick cooking spray.

2 Whisk eggs, half-and-half, Italian seasoning, salt and pepper in medium bowl until well blended. Stir in spinach and cheese; mix well. Pour into prepared pan.

3 Bake 33 minutes or until toothpick inserted into center comes out clean. Remove to wire rack; cool 10 minutes before serving.

tip

To remove quiche from pan for serving, run knife around edge of pan to loosen. Invert quiche onto plate; invert again onto second plate. Cut into wedges to serve.

asparagus frittata prosciutto cups

makes 6 servings (12 cups)

1 tablespoon olive oil

1 small red onion, finely chopped

1½ cups sliced asparagus (½-inch pieces)

1 clove garlic, minced

12 thin slices prosciutto

8 eggs

½ cup (2 ounces) grated white Cheddar cheese

¼ cup grated Parmesan cheese

2 tablespoons milk

⅛ teaspoon black pepper

1 Preheat oven to 375°F. Spray 12 standard (2½-inch) muffin cups with nonstick cooking spray.

2 Heat oil in large skillet over medium heat. Add onion; cook and stir 4 minutes or until softened. Add asparagus and garlic; cook and stir 8 minutes or until asparagus is crisp-tender. Set aside to cool slightly.

3 Line each prepared muffin cup with prosciutto slice. (Prosciutto should cover cup as much as possible, with edges extending above muffin pan.) Whisk eggs, Cheddar, Parmesan, milk and pepper in large bowl until well blended. Stir in asparagus mixture until blended. Pour into prosciutto-lined cups, filling about three-fourths full.

4 Bake about 20 minutes or until frittatas are puffed and golden brown and edges are pulling away from pan. Cool in pan 10 minutes; remove to wire rack. Serve warm or at room temperature.

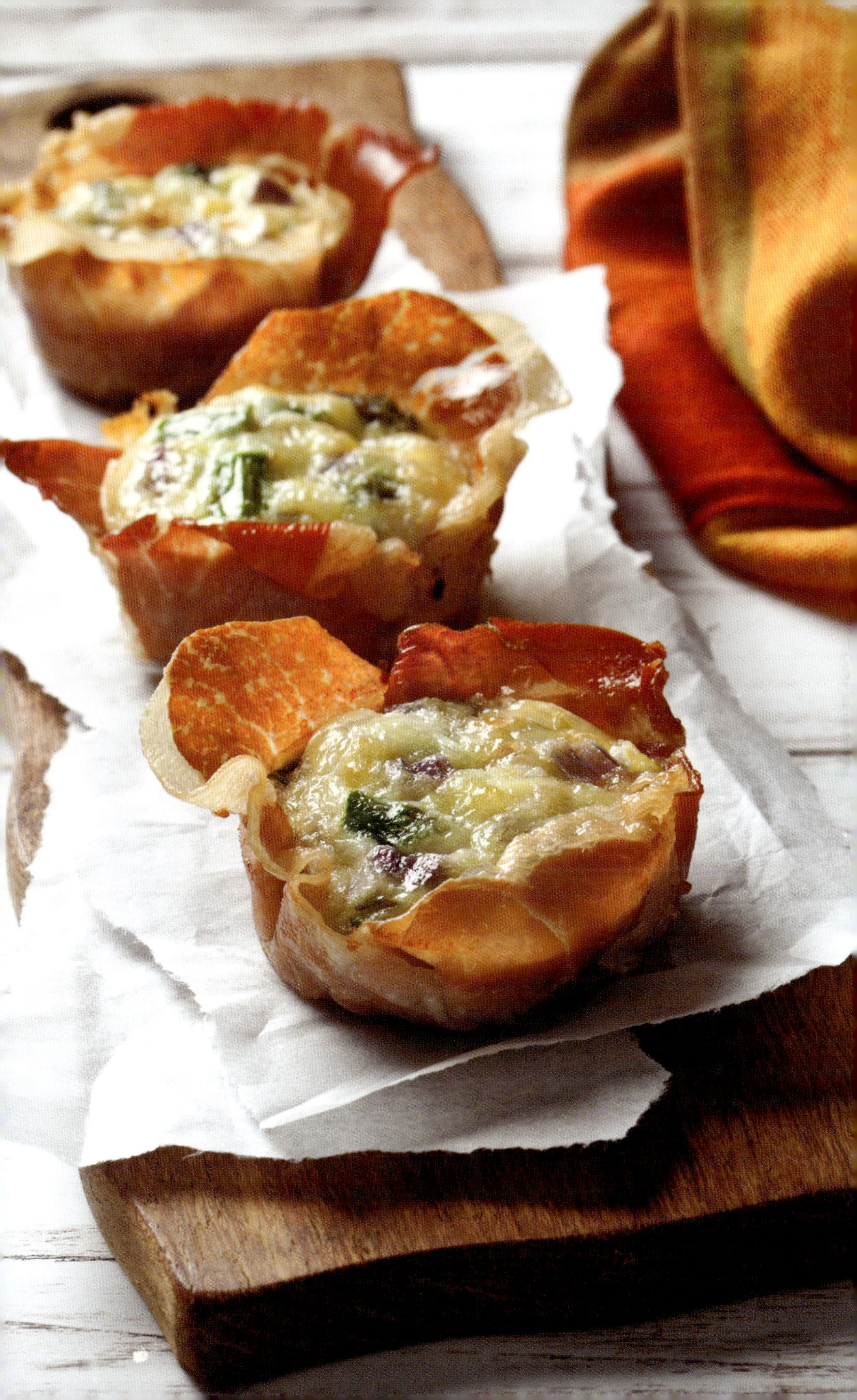

bacon and potato quiche

makes 8 servings

1 refrigerated pie crust (half of 15-ounce package)

12 ounces thick-cut bacon, cut crosswise into ½-inch pieces

8 ounces Yukon Gold potatoes, peeled and cut into ¼-inch pieces

1 small onion, chopped

½ teaspoon chopped fresh thyme

1½ cups half-and-half

4 eggs

½ teaspoon salt

½ teaspoon black pepper

¾ cup (3 ounces) shredded Dubliner or white Cheddar cheese

2 tablespoons chopped fresh chives

1 Preheat oven to 450°F. Line baking sheet with foil.

2 Roll out pie crust into 12-inch circle on floured surface. Line 9-inch pie plate with crust, pressing firmly into bottom and up side of plate. Trim crust to leave 1-inch overhang; fold under and flute edge. Prick bottom of crust with fork. Bake about 8 minutes or until lightly browned. Remove to wire rack to cool slightly. *Reduce oven temperature to 375°F.*

3 Cook bacon in large skillet over medium heat about 10 minutes or until crisp, stirring occasionally. Drain on paper towel-lined plate. Drain all but 1 tablespoon drippings from skillet. Add potatoes, onion and thyme to skillet; cook about 10 minutes or until vegetables are tender, stirring occasionally.

4 Place pie plate on prepared baking sheet. Whisk half-and-half, eggs, salt and pepper in medium bowl until well blended. Sprinkle cheese evenly over bottom of crust; top with vegetable mixture. Pour in egg mixture; sprinkle with chives.

5 Bake 35 to 40 minutes or until quiche is set and knife inserted into center comes out clean. Let stand 10 minutes before slicing.

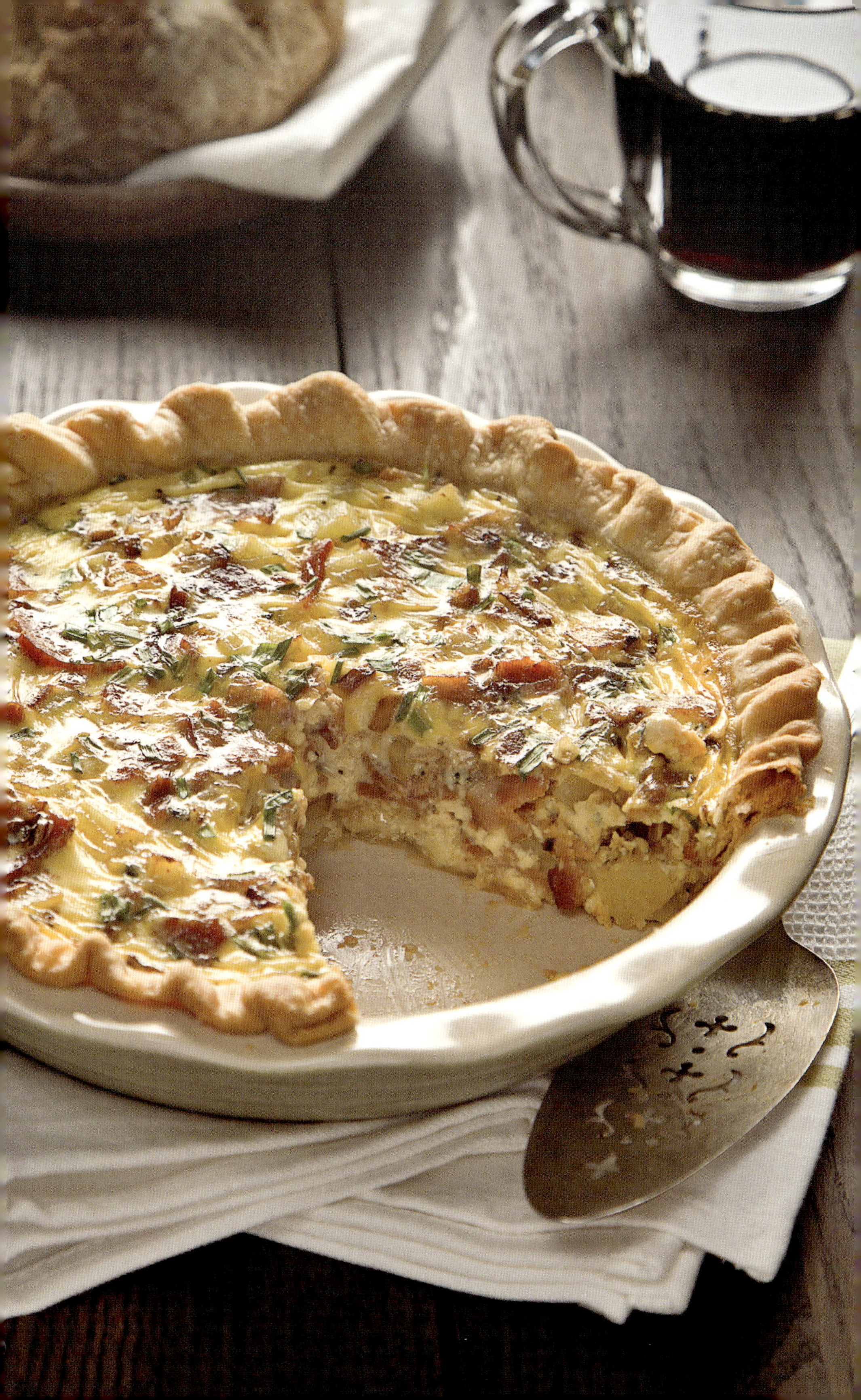

zucchini-tomato frittata

makes 4 servings

1 tablespoon olive oil

1 cup sliced zucchini

1 cup broccoli florets

1 cup diced red or yellow bell pepper

6 eggs

½ cup cottage cheese

½ cup rehydrated* sun-dried tomatoes (1 ounce dry), coarsely chopped

¼ cup chopped green onions

¼ cup chopped fresh basil

½ teaspoon salt

⅛ teaspoon ground red pepper

2 tablespoons grated Parmesan cheese

Paprika (optional)

*To rehydrate sun-dried tomatoes, pour 1 cup boiling water over tomatoes in small bowl. Let soak 5 to 10 minutes or until softened; drain well.

1 Preheat broiler. Heat oil in 10-inch ovenproof skillet over medium-high heat. Add zucchini, broccoli and bell pepper; cook and stir 3 to 4 minutes or until vegetables are crisp-tender.

2 Whisk eggs, cottage cheese, sun-dried tomatoes, green onions, basil, salt and ground red pepper in medium bowl until well blended.

3 Pour egg mixture over vegetables in skillet. Cook 7 to 8 minutes or until frittata is almost firm and golden brown on bottom, gently lifting edges so uncooked portion flows underneath. Remove from heat; sprinkle with Parmesan.

4 Broil about 5 inches from heat about 3 minutes or until golden brown. Garnish with paprika. Cut into four wedges.

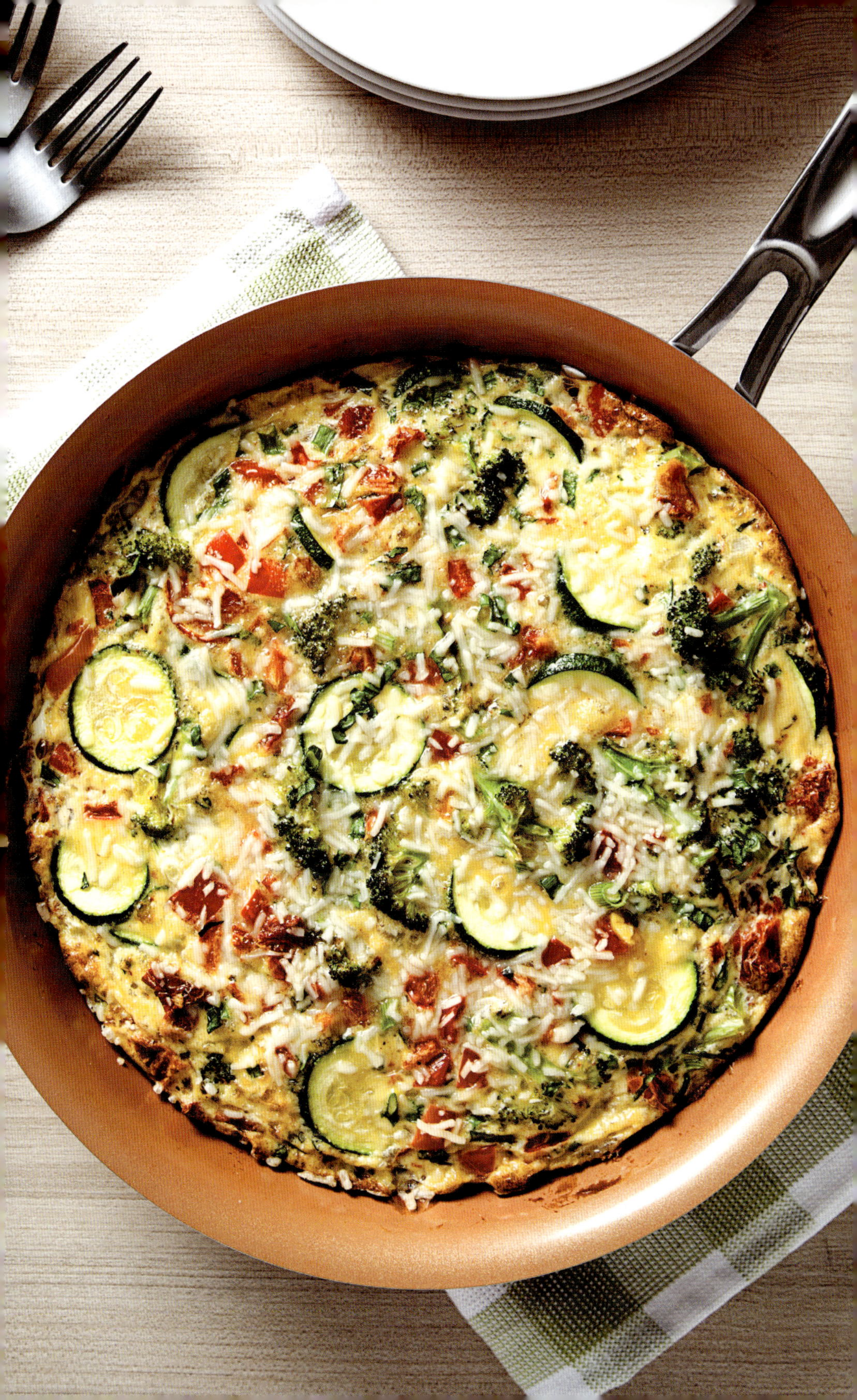

individual spinach and bacon quiches

makes 6 servings (12 mini quiches)

3 slices bacon

½ small onion, diced

1 package (10 ounces) frozen chopped spinach, thawed and squeezed dry

½ teaspoon black pepper

⅛ teaspoon ground nutmeg

Pinch salt

3 eggs, lightly beaten

1 container (15 ounces) whole-milk ricotta cheese

2 cups (8 ounces) shredded mozzarella cheese

1 cup grated Parmesan cheese

1 Preheat oven to 350°F. Spray 12 standard (2½-inch) muffin cups with nonstick cooking spray.

2 Cook bacon in large skillet over medium-high heat until crisp. Drain on paper towel-lined plate until cool enough to handle. Crumble bacon.

3 Heat same skillet with bacon drippings over medium heat. Add onion; cook and stir 5 minutes or until tender. Add spinach, pepper, nutmeg and salt; cook and stir 3 minutes or until liquid is evaporated. Remove from heat. Stir in bacon; set aside to cool.

4 Whisk eggs in large bowl. Add ricotta, mozzarella and Parmesan; stir until well blended. Add cooled spinach mixture; mix well. Spoon evenly into prepared muffin cups.

5 Bake 40 minutes or until set. Cool in pan 10 minutes. Run thin knife around edges to remove from pan. Serve immediately.

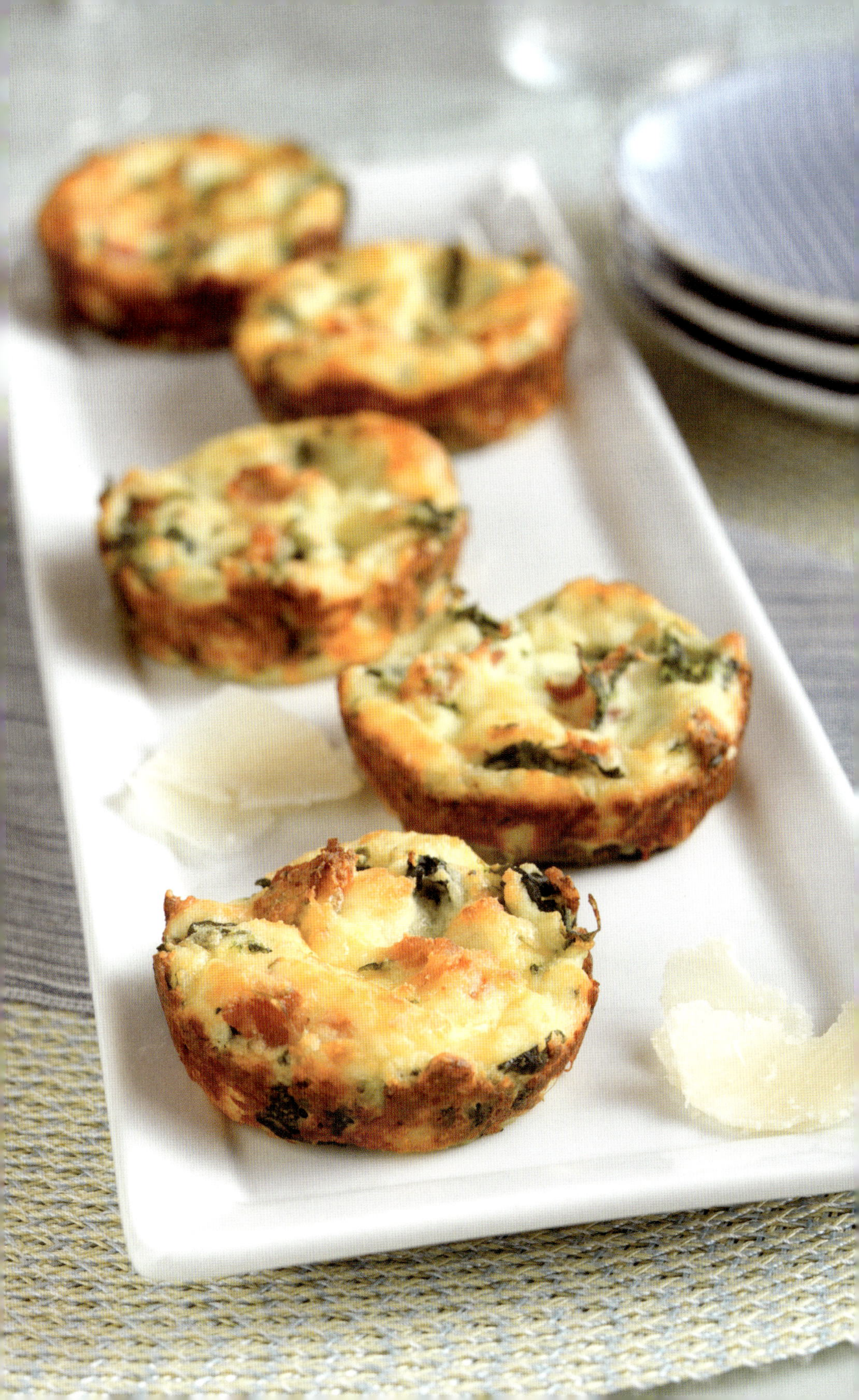

vegetable quinoa frittata

makes 6 servings

1 tablespoon olive oil

1 cup diced onion

1 cup small broccoli florets

¾ cup finely chopped red bell pepper

2 cloves garlic, minced

1¼ teaspoons kosher salt

⅛ teaspoon black pepper

1½ cups cooked quinoa

¼ cup sun-dried tomatoes, chopped

8 eggs, lightly beaten

¼ cup grated Parmesan cheese

1 Preheat oven to 400°F.

2 Heat oil in large ovenproof nonstick skillet over medium-high heat. Add onion and broccoli; cook and stir 4 minutes, Add bell pepper; cook and stir 2 minutes. Add garlic, salt and black pepper; cook and stir 30 seconds. Stir in quinoa and sun-dried tomatoes.

3 Gently stir in eggs; cook until softly scrambled. Sprinkle with cheese.

4 Bake about 7 minutes or until eggs are set. Let stand 5 minutes before cutting into wedges.

edamame frittata

makes 4 servings

2 tablespoons olive oil

½ cup frozen shelled edamame

⅓ cup frozen corn

¼ cup chopped shallot (1 shallot)

5 eggs

¾ teaspoon Italian seasoning

½ teaspoon salt

½ teaspoon black pepper

¼ cup chopped green onions

½ cup crumbled goat cheese

1 Preheat broiler. Heat oil in large ovenproof nonstick skillet over medium-high heat. Add edamame, corn and shallot; cook and stir 6 to 8 minutes or until shallot is lightly browned and edamame are hot.

2 Meanwhile, whisk eggs, Italian seasoning, salt and pepper in medium bowl until well blended. Stir in green onions.

3 Pour egg mixture over vegetables in skillet. Sprinkle with cheese. Cook over medium heat 5 to 7 minutes or until eggs are set on bottom, gently lifting edges to allow uncooked portion to flow underneath.

4 Broil 6 inches from heat 1 minute or until top is puffy and golden brown. Loosen frittata from skillet with spatula; slide onto small platter or plate. Cut into wedges.

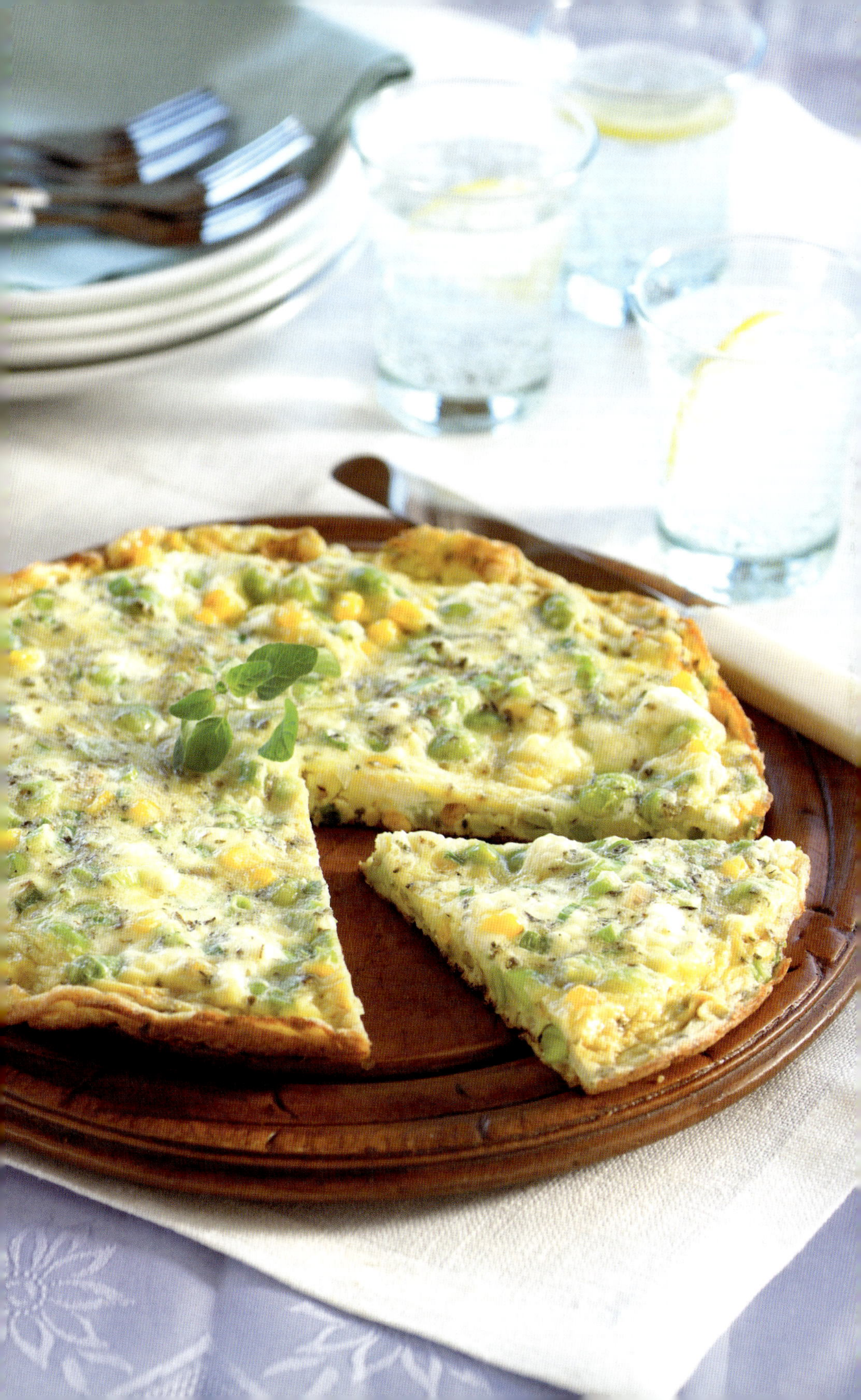

chile corn quiche

makes 6 servings

1 unbaked 9-inch
  pie crust
1 can (8¾ ounces)
  whole kernel corn,
  drained, *or* 1 cup
  frozen whole kernel
  corn, cooked
1 can (4 ounces) diced
  mild green chiles,
  drained
¼ cup thinly sliced
  green onions
1 cup (4 ounces)
  shredded Monterey
  Jack cheese
1½ cups half-and-half
3 eggs
½ teaspoon salt
½ teaspoon ground
  cumin

1 Preheat oven to 450°F. Line crust
  with foil; fill with dried beans or
  uncooked rice. Bake 10 minutes.
  Remove foil and beans; bake
  5 minutes or until lightly browned.
  Cool on wire rack. *Reduce oven
  temperature to 375°F.*

2 Combine corn, chiles and green
  onions in small bowl; mix well.
  Spoon into crust; top with cheese.

3 Whisk half-and-half, eggs, salt and
  cumin in medium bowl until well
  blended. Pour over cheese.

4 Bake 35 to 45 minutes or until
  filling is puffed and knife inserted
  into center comes out clean. Let
  stand 10 minutes before serving.

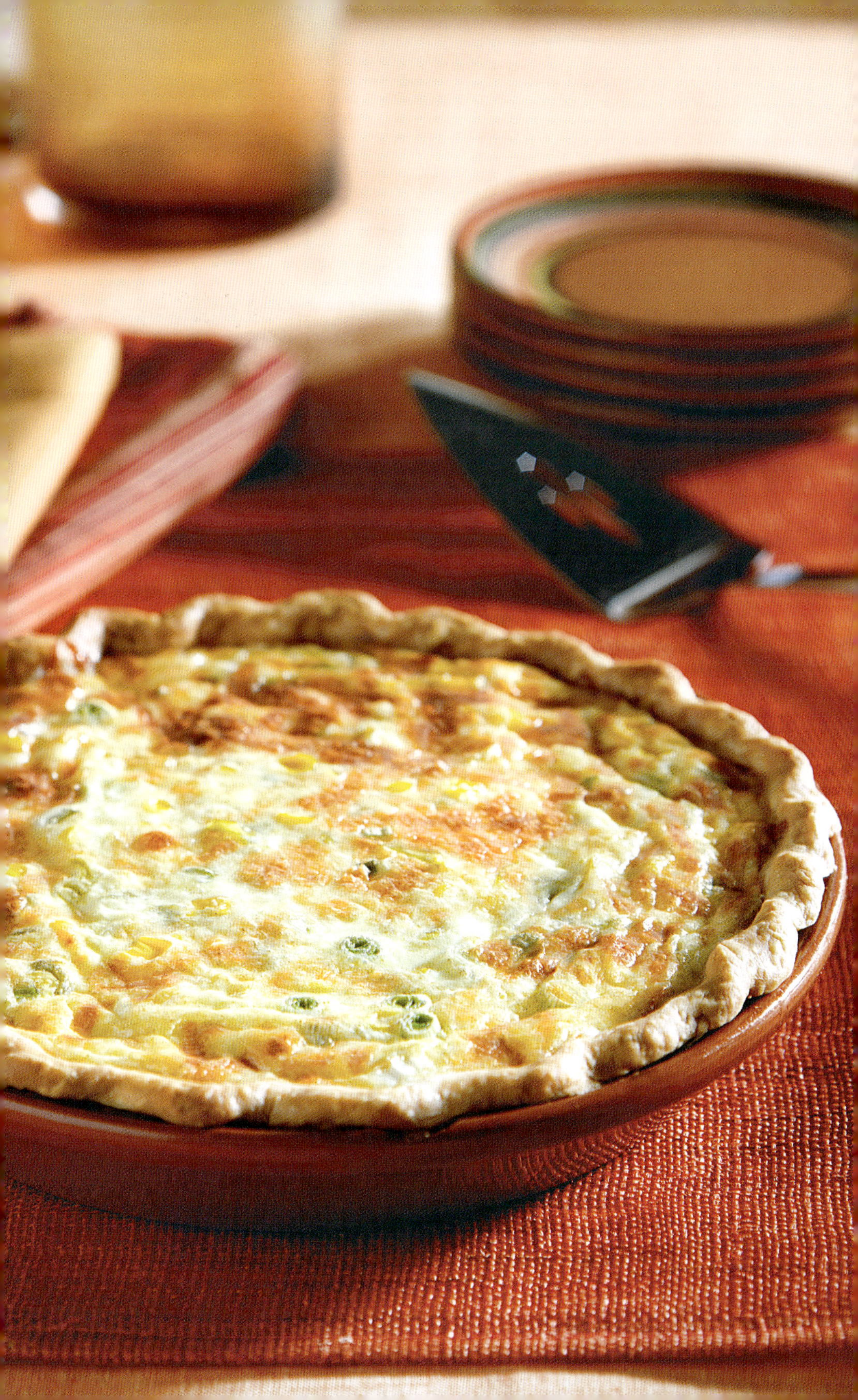

mediterranean frittata

makes 6 to 8 appetizer servings

¼ cup extra virgin olive oil

5 small onions, thinly sliced

1 can (about 14 ounces) whole tomatoes, drained and chopped

4 ounces prosciutto or cooked ham, chopped

¼ cup grated Parmesan cheese

2 tablespoons chopped fresh parsley

½ teaspoon dried marjoram

¼ teaspoon salt

¼ teaspoon dried basil

⅛ teaspoon black pepper

6 eggs

2 tablespoons butter

1 Heat oil in large skillet over medium-high heat. Add onions; cook and stir 8 to 10 minutes until soft and golden. Reduce heat to medium. Stir in tomatoes; cook 5 minutes. Remove vegetables to large bowl with slotted spoon; discard drippings. Cool to room temperature.

2 Stir prosciutto, Parmesan, parsley, marjoram, salt, basil and pepper into tomato mixture. Whisk eggs in medium bowl; stir into prosciutto mixture.

3 Preheat broiler. Heat butter in medium ovenproof nonstick skillet over medium heat until melted and bubbly. Reduce heat to low; add egg mixture to skillet, spreading evenly. Cook 8 to 10 minutes until all but top ¼ inch of frittata is set. (Shake skillet gently to test.) *Do not stir.*

4 Broil frittata about 4 inches from heat 1 to 2 minutes or until top is set. (Do not brown or frittata will be dry.) Serve warm or at room temperature. Cut into wedges.

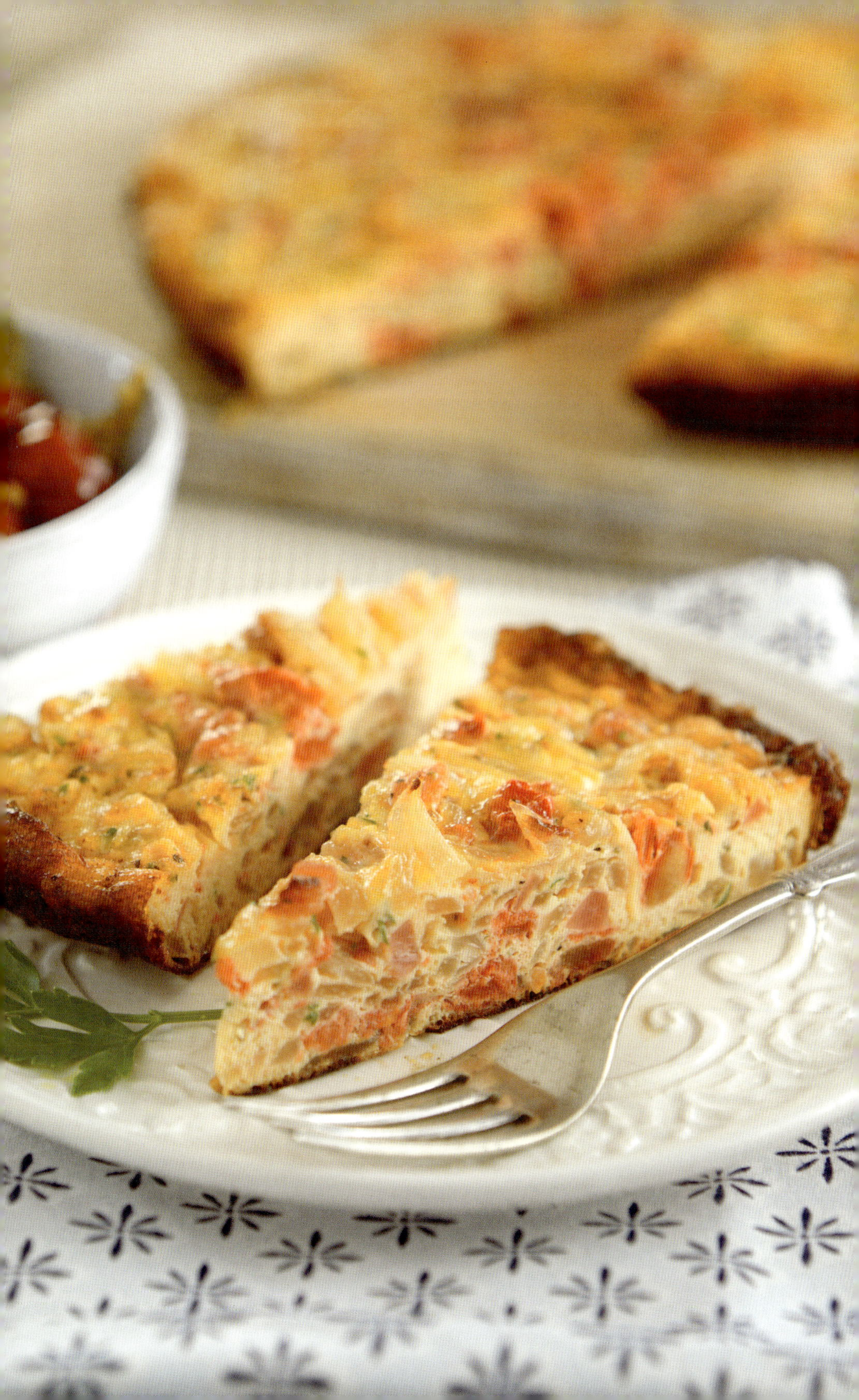

mini spinach frittatas

makes 6 servings (12 mini frittatas)

1 tablespoon olive oil

½ cup chopped onion

8 eggs

¼ cup plain yogurt

1 package (10 ounces) frozen chopped spinach, thawed and squeezed dry

½ cup (2 ounces) shredded white Cheddar cheese

¼ cup grated Parmesan cheese

¾ teaspoon salt

⅛ teaspoon black pepper

⅛ teaspoon ground red pepper

Dash ground nutmeg

1 Preheat oven to 350°F. Spray 12 standard (2½-inch) muffin cups with nonstick cooking spray.

2 Heat oil in large nonstick skillet over medium heat. Add onion; cook and stir about 5 minutes or until tender. Set aside to cool slightly.

3 Whisk eggs and yogurt in large bowl. Stir in spinach, Cheddar, Parmesan, salt, black pepper, red pepper, nutmeg and onion until blended. Divide mixture evenly among prepared muffin cups.

4 Bake 20 to 25 minutes or until eggs are puffed and firm and no longer shiny. Cool in pan 2 minutes. Loosen bottom and sides with small spatula or knife; remove to wire rack. Serve warm or at room temperature.

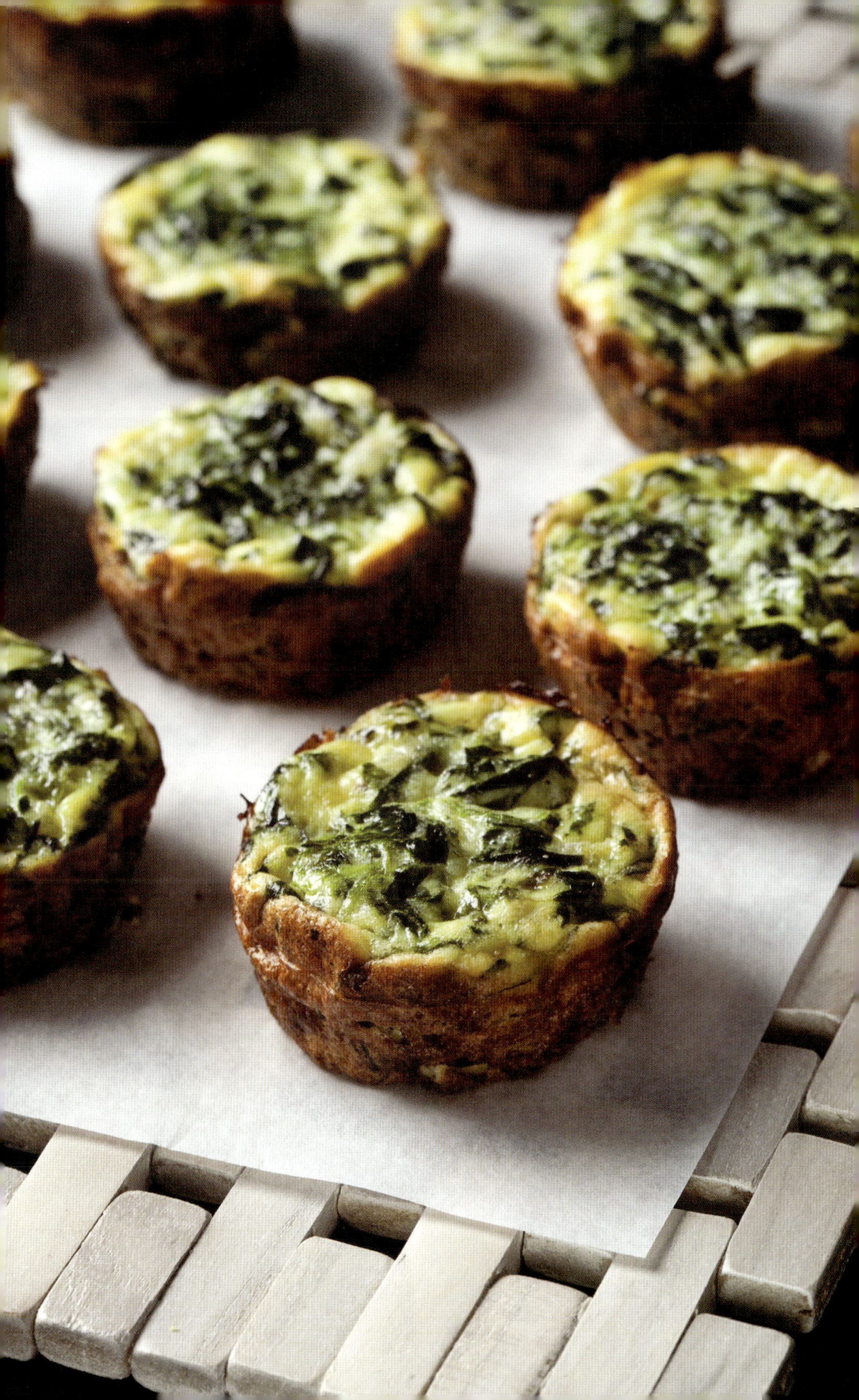

eggs in the oven

roasted pepper and sourdough brunch casserole

makes 8 servings

3 cups sourdough bread cubes

1 jar (12 ounces) roasted red pepper strips, drained

1 cup (4 ounces) shredded sharp Cheddar cheese

1 cup (4 ounces) shredded Monterey Jack cheese

1 cup cottage cheese

6 eggs

1 cup milk

¼ cup chopped fresh cilantro

¼ teaspoon black pepper

1 Spray 11×7-inch baking dish with nonstick cooking spray. Place bread cubes in prepared baking dish. Arrange roasted peppers evenly over bread cubes; sprinkle with Cheddar and Monterey Jack.

2 Place cottage cheese in food processor or blender; process until smooth. Add eggs and milk; process just until blended. Pour over ingredients in baking dish; sprinkle with cilantro and black pepper. Cover and refrigerate 4 hours or overnight.

3 Preheat oven to 375°F. Bake, uncovered, 40 minutes or until center is set and top is golden brown.

bacon and egg cups

makes 12 servings

12 slices bacon, crisp-cooked and cut crosswise into thirds
6 eggs
½ cup diced red and green bell pepper
½ cup (2 ounces) shredded pepper jack cheese
½ cup half-and-half
¼ teaspoon salt
¼ teaspoon black pepper

1 Preheat oven to 350°F. Lightly spray 12 standard (2½-inch) muffin cups with nonstick cooking spray.

2 Place 3 bacon slices in each prepared muffin cup, overlapping in bottom.

3 Whisk eggs, bell pepper, cheese, half-and-half, salt and black pepper in medium bowl until well blended. Fill each muffin cup with ¼ cup egg mixture.

4 Bake 20 to 25 minutes or until eggs are set in center. Run knife around edge of each cup to loosen before removing from pan.

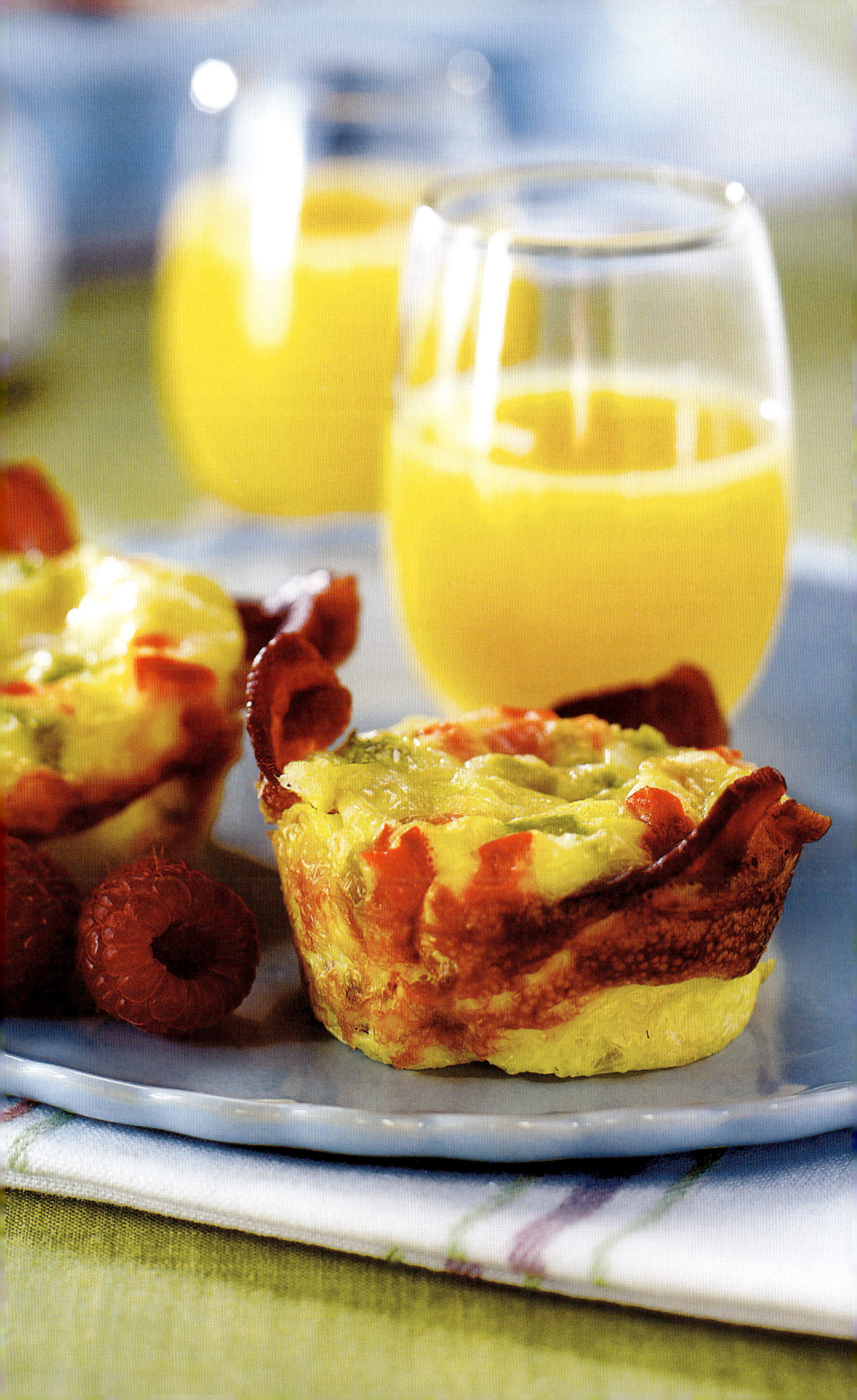

breakfast pizza margherita

makes 6 servings

1 (12-inch) prepared
    pizza crust

3 slices bacon or
    turkey bacon

8 eggs

½ cup milk

1½ tablespoons
    chopped fresh
    basil, divided

¼ teaspoon salt

⅛ teaspoon black
    pepper

2 plum tomatoes,
    thinly sliced

½ cup (2 ounces)
    shredded
    mozzarella cheese

¼ cup (1 ounce)
    shredded Cheddar
    cheese

1 Preheat oven to 450°F. Place pizza crust on 12-inch pizza pan. Bake 6 to 8 minutes or until heated through.

2 Meanwhile, cook bacon in large nonstick skillet over medium-high heat until crisp. Drain on paper towel-lined plate. Crumble bacon.

3 Whisk eggs, milk, ½ tablespoon basil, salt and pepper in medium bowl until well blended.

4 Add egg mixture to skillet; cook over medium heat until eggs begin to set around edges. Gently stir, allowing uncooked portion to flow underneath. Repeat stirring every 1 to 2 minutes or just until eggs are set. Remove from heat.

5 Arrange tomato slices on warmed pizza crust. Spoon scrambled eggs over tomatoes; sprinkle with bacon and cheeses. Bake 1 minute or until cheeses are melted. Sprinkle with remaining 1 tablespoon basil.

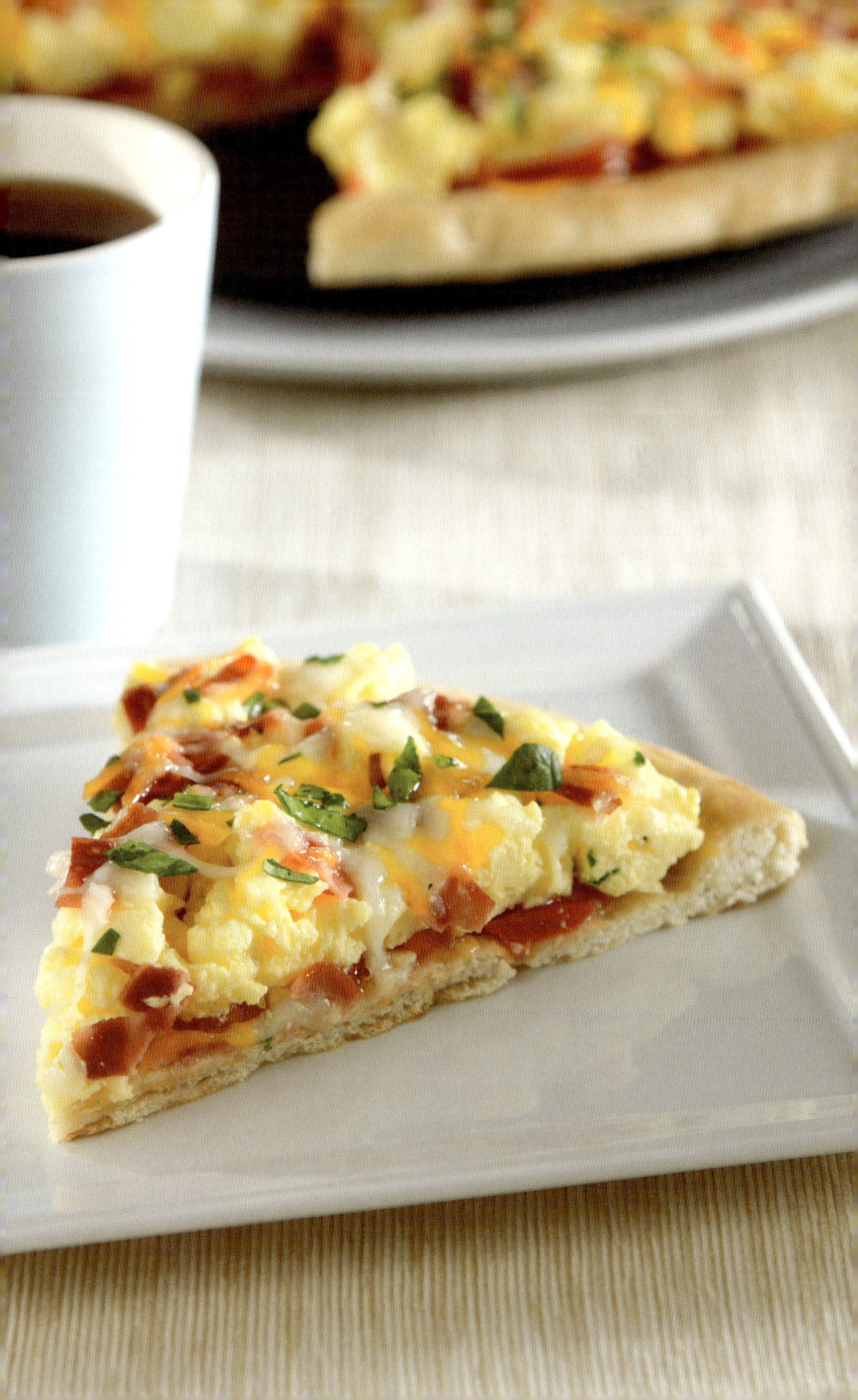

spinach soufflé

makes 4 servings

1 pound fresh spinach leaves

¼ cup (½ stick) butter

1 tablespoon finely chopped shallot

¼ cup all-purpose flour

¼ teaspoon salt

¼ teaspoon ground nutmeg

⅛ teaspoon ground white pepper

1½ cups milk, warmed to room temperature

6 eggs, separated

½ cup grated Parmesan cheese

Pinch cream of tartar (optional)

1 Preheat oven to 375°F. Grease 2-quart soufflé dish or deep casserole.

2 Bring large saucepan of salted water to a boil over high heat. Add spinach; cook 1 to 2 minutes or just until wilted. Drain and immediately plunge into cold water to stop cooking. When cool enough to handle, squeeze out excess moisture and finely chop spinach. (You should have about 1 cup.)

3 Melt butter in large saucepan over medium heat. Add shallot; cook and stir 2 to 3 minutes. Stir in flour, salt, nutmeg and pepper. Gradually add milk; cook and stir until mixture comes to a boil and thickens. Let cool slightly. Stir in egg yolks until well blended. Add spinach and cheese; mix well.

4 Combine egg whites and cream of tartar, if desired, in large bowl; beat with electric mixer at high speed until stiff peaks form. Gently fold egg whites into spinach mixture until almost combined. (Some white streaks should remain.) Transfer mixture to prepared soufflé dish.

5 Bake 30 to 40 minutes or until puffed and golden. (Wooden skewer inserted into center should come out moist but clean.) Serve immediately.

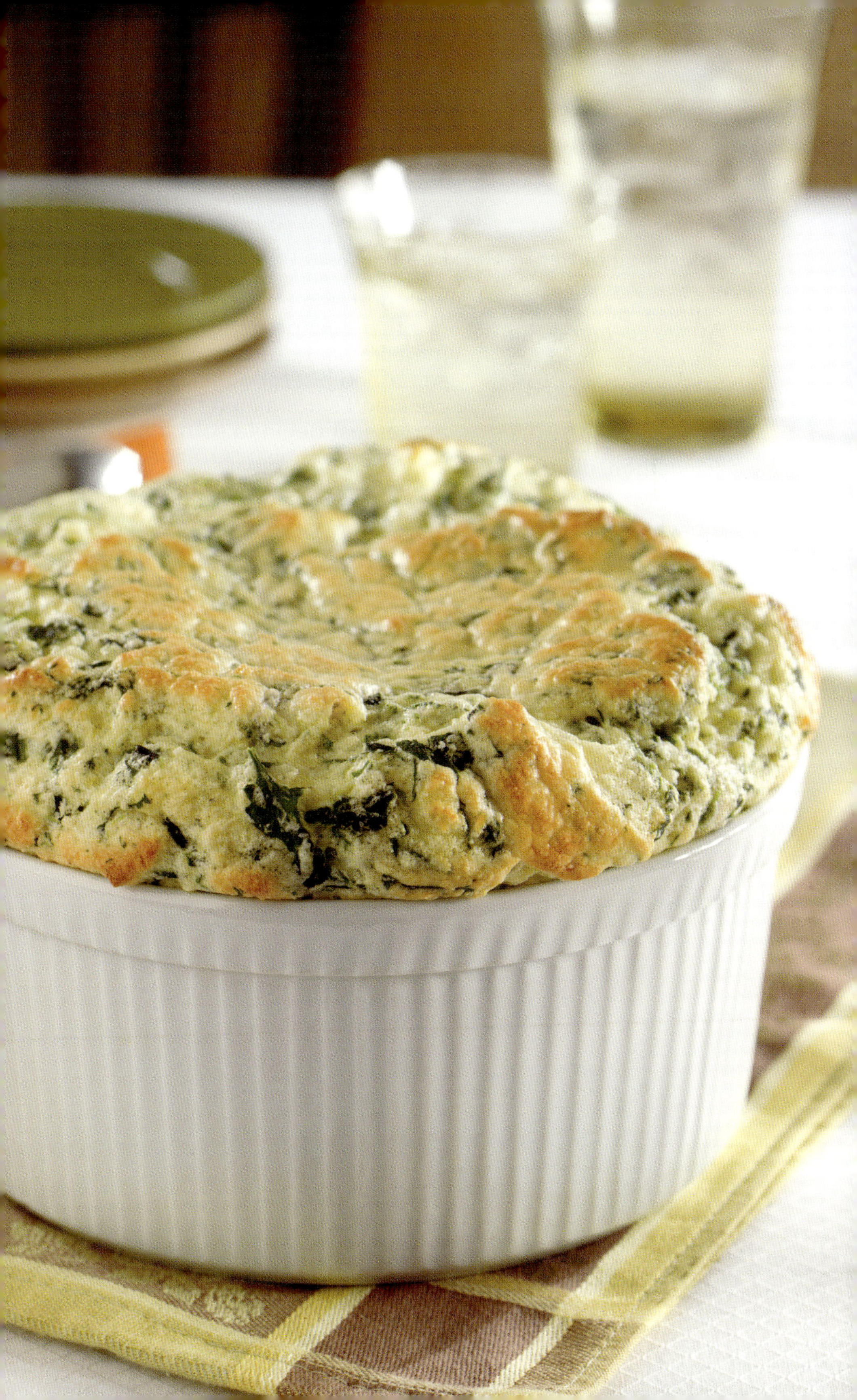

german apple pancake

makes 6 servings

1 tablespoon butter

1 large *or* 2 small apples, peeled and thinly sliced (about 1½ cups)

1 tablespoon packed brown sugar

1½ teaspoons ground cinnamon, divided

2 eggs

2 egg whites

1 tablespoon granulated sugar

1 teaspoon vanilla

¼ teaspoon salt

½ cup all-purpose flour

½ cup milk

Maple syrup (optional)

1 Preheat oven to 425°F.

2 Melt butter in medium cast iron or other ovenproof skillet over medium heat. Add apples, brown sugar and ½ teaspoon cinnamon; cook and stir 5 minutes or until apples just begin to soften. Remove from heat. Arrange apple slices in single layer in skillet.

3 Whisk eggs, egg whites, granulated sugar, remaining 1 teaspoon cinnamon, vanilla and salt in medium bowl until well blended. Stir in flour and milk until smooth and well blended. Pour batter evenly over apples.

4 Bake 20 to 25 minutes or until puffed and golden brown. Serve with maple syrup, if desired.

note

Pancake will fall slightly after being removed from the oven.

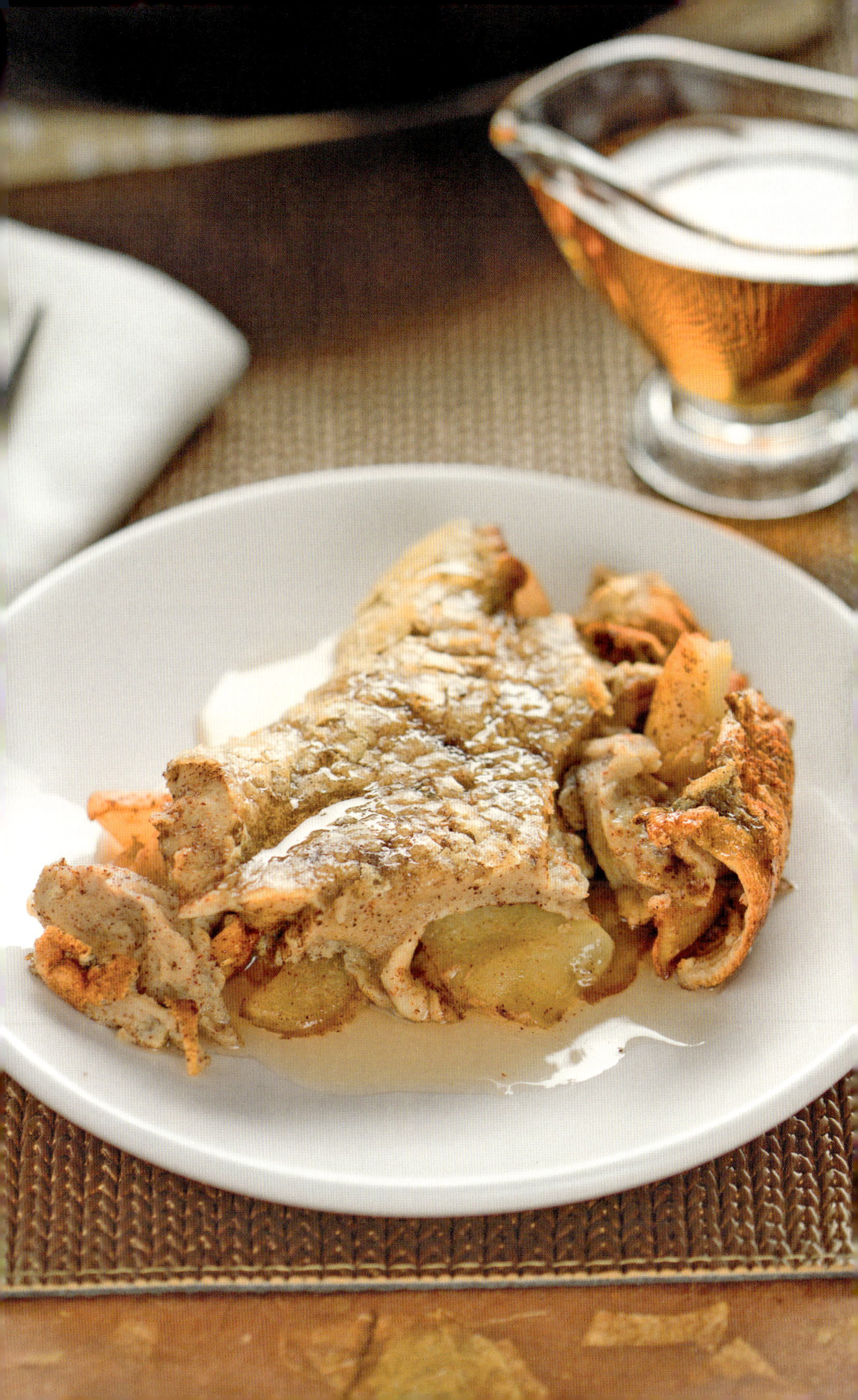

breakfast flats

makes 4 servings

8 slices bacon,
   chopped

1 package (14 ounces)
   refrigerated pizza
   dough

   All-purpose flour,
   for dusting

1½ cups (6 ounces)
    shredded Cheddar
    cheese

4 eggs

   Salt and black
   pepper

1 Preheat oven to 400°F. Line two baking sheets with parchment paper.

2 Cook bacon in large nonstick skillet over medium-high heat about 8 minutes or until crisp, stirring occasionally. Drain on paper towel-lined plate. (Reserve bacon drippings in skillet to cook eggs, if desired.)

3 Divide pizza dough into four equal pieces. Roll out each piece into 8½×4-inch rectangle on lightly floured surface; round corners slightly. Place dough on prepared baking sheets; top with cheese and bacon.

4 Bake 10 minutes or until crust is golden brown and crisp and cheese is melted.

5 Meanwhile, heat skillet with bacon drippings over medium heat. (If there is more than 1 tablespoon drippings, drain off excess. Or wipe out skillet with paper towels and spray with nonstick cooking spray.) Cook eggs sunny-side up. Top baked crusts with fried eggs; season with salt and pepper. Serve immediately.

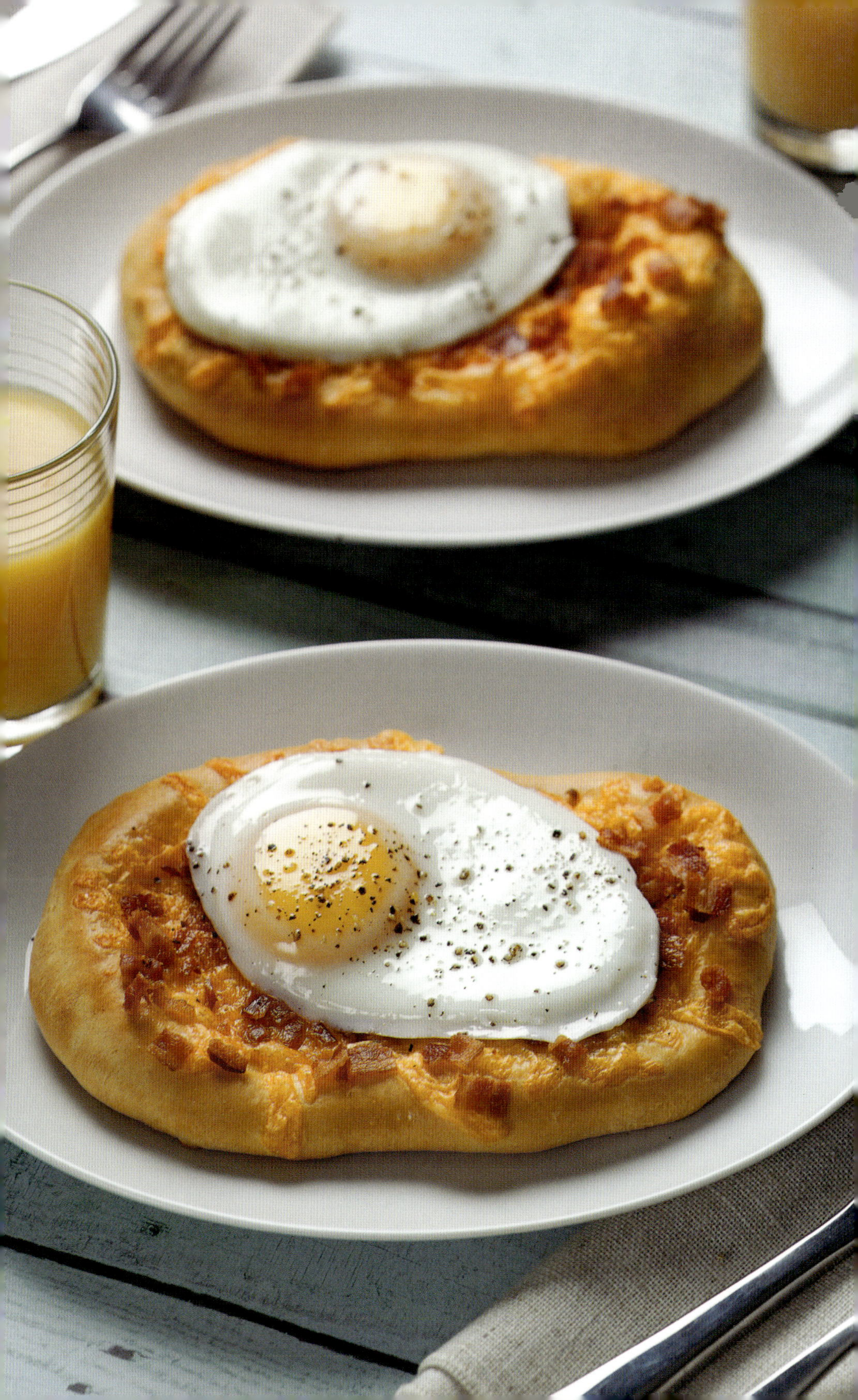

cheddar and leek strata

makes 12 servings

8 eggs

2 cups milk

½ cup porter ale
or stout

2 cloves garlic, minced

¼ teaspoon salt

¼ teaspoon black
pepper

1 loaf (16 ounces)
sourdough bread,
cut into ½-inch
cubes

2 small leeks, coarsely
chopped

1 red bell pepper,
chopped

1½ cups (6 ounces)
shredded Swiss
cheese

1½ cups (6 ounces)
shredded sharp
Cheddar cheese

1 Spray 13×9-inch baking dish with nonstick cooking spray. Whisk eggs, milk, ale, garlic, salt and black pepper in large bowl until well blended.

2 Spread half of bread cubes in prepared baking dish; sprinkle with half of leeks and half of bell pepper. Top with ¾ cup Swiss and ¾ cup Cheddar. Repeat layers. Pour egg mixture evenly over top.

3 Cover tightly with plastic wrap or foil. Weigh down top of strata with slightly smaller baking dish. Refrigerate at least 2 hours or overnight.

4 Preheat oven to 350°F. Bake, uncovered, 40 to 45 minutes or until center is set. Serve immediately.

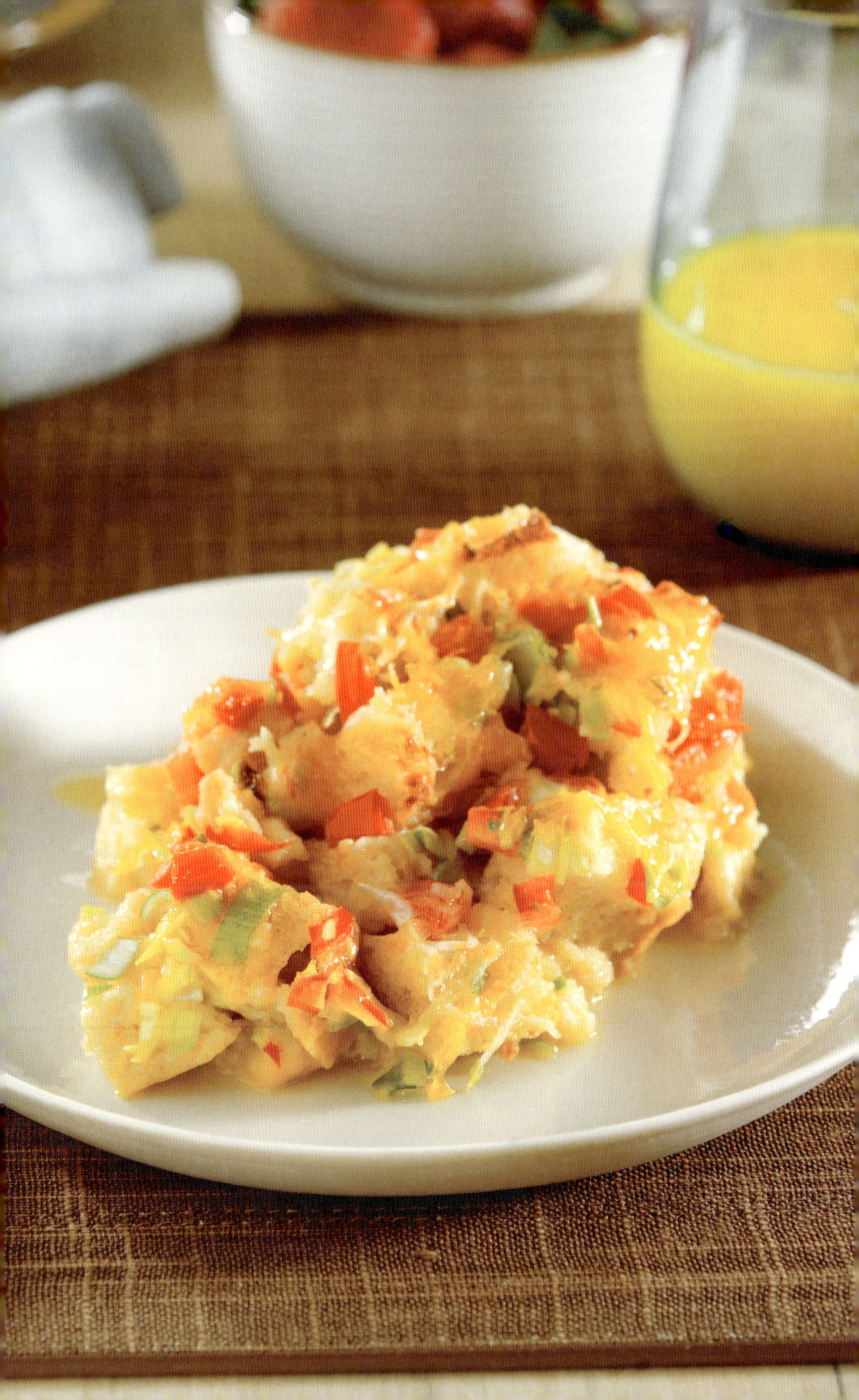

breakfast biscuit bake

makes 8 servings

8 ounces bacon, chopped

1 small onion, finely chopped

1 clove garlic, minced

¼ teaspoon red pepper flakes

5 eggs

¼ cup milk

½ cup (2 ounces) shredded white Cheddar cheese, divided

¼ teaspoon salt

⅛ teaspoon black pepper

1 package (16 ounces) refrigerated jumbo buttermilk biscuits (8 biscuits)

1 Preheat oven to 425°F. Cook bacon in large cast iron skillet until crisp. Remove to paper towel-lined plate. Drain off and reserve drippings, leaving 1 tablespoon in skillet.

2 Add onion, garlic and red pepper flakes to skillet; cook over medium heat 8 minutes or until onion is softened, stirring occasionally. Set aside to cool slightly.

3 Whisk eggs, milk, ¼ cup cheese, salt and black pepper in medium bowl until well blended. Stir in onion mixture.

4 Wipe out any onion mixture remaining in skillet; grease with additional drippings, if necessary. Separate biscuits and arrange in single layer in bottom of skillet. (Bottom of skillet should be completely covered.) Pour egg mixture over biscuits; sprinkle with remaining ¼ cup cheese and cooked bacon.

5 Bake about 25 minutes or until puffed and golden brown. Serve warm.

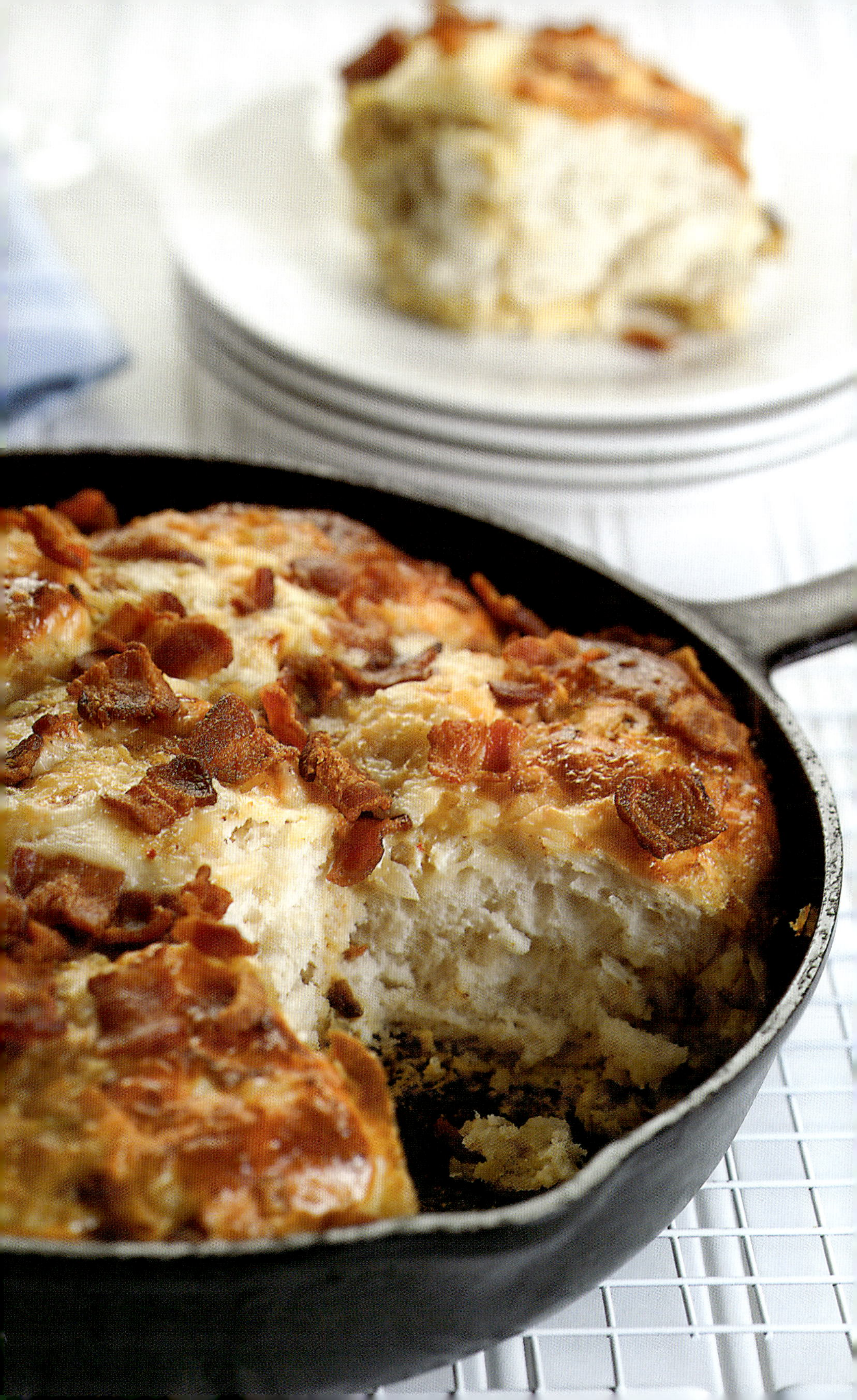

eggs benedict cups

makes 3 servings (6 cups)

6 **English muffin tops**
6 **thin slices Canadian
    bacon**
6 **eggs**
  **Salt and black
    pepper**
3 **egg yolks**
¼ **cup water**
2 **tablespoons
    lemon juice**
½ **cup (1 stick) cold
    butter, cut into
    8 pieces**

1 Preheat oven to 350°F. Spray
  six jumbo (3½-inch) muffin cups
  with nonstick cooking spray.*

2 Press English muffins into
  prepared cups. Top with Canadian
  bacon, pressing down into muffins
  as much as possible. Crack one
  egg into each cup. Sprinkle with
  salt and pepper.

3 Bake 10 to 12 minutes or until
  eggs reach desired doneness
  (eggs whites may not look
  completely set). Remove from
  pan to serving plates.

4 While eggs are baking, prepare
  hollandaise sauce. Combine egg
  yolks, water and lemon juice in
  small saucepan; cook over low
  heat about 4 minutes or until
  mixture begins to bubble around
  edges, whisking constantly. Whisk
  in butter, 1 piece at a time, until
  butter is melted and sauce has
  thickened. (Do not allow sauce
  to boil.) Whisk in ¼ teaspoon salt.
  Serve sauce immediately with egg
  cups.

*If you don't have jumbo-size muffin
cups, standard (2½-inch) muffin
cups can be used instead. Prepare as
directed—the ingredients will fit into
the cups but it is a much tighter fit.*

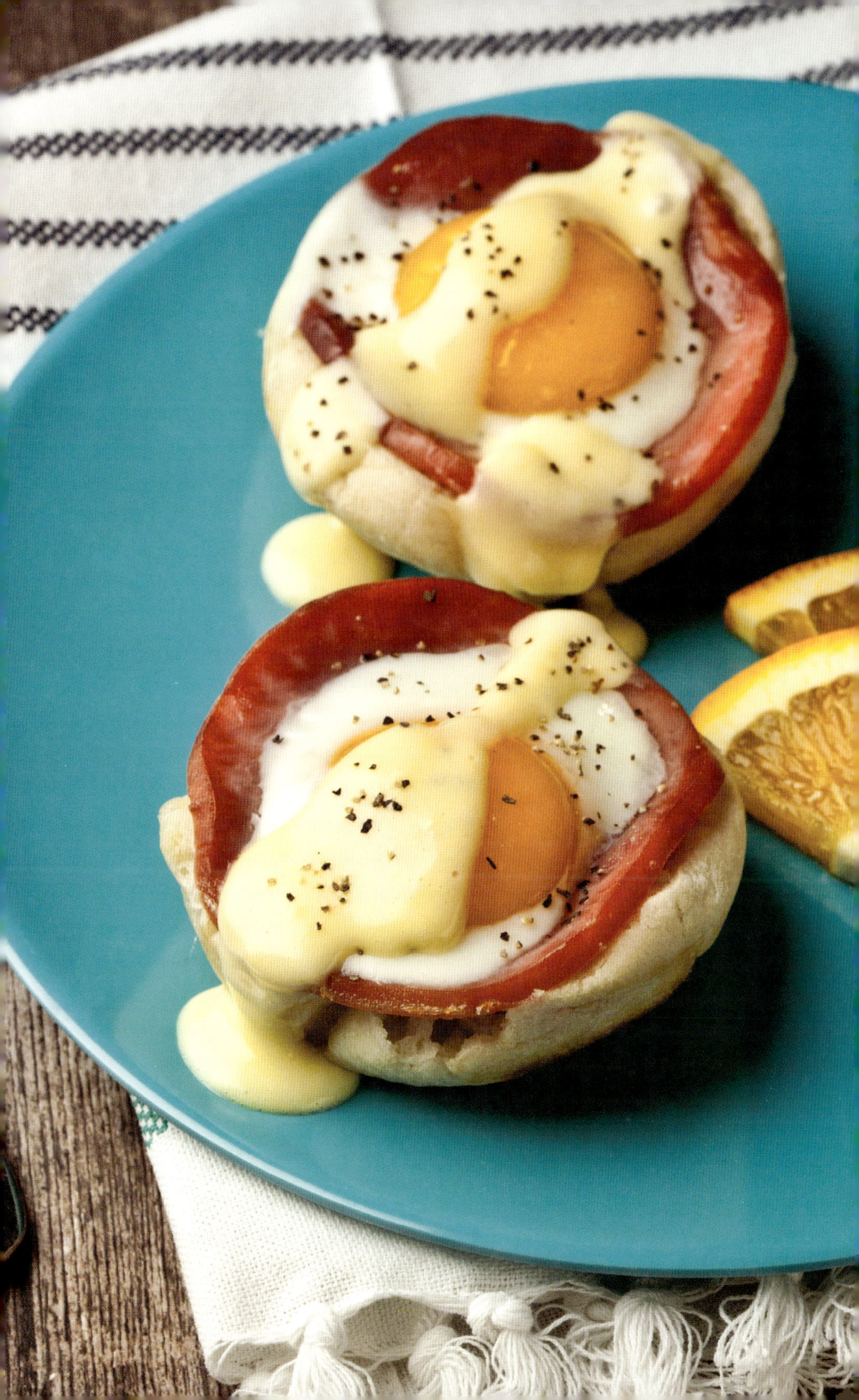

dutch baby pancake

makes 2 servings

3 tablespoons butter, divided, plus additional for serving

½ cup all-purpose flour

2 tablespoons granulated sugar

¼ teaspoon salt

½ cup whole milk, at room temperature

2 eggs, at room temperature

¼ teaspoon vanilla

Powdered sugar

Lemon wedges

1 Preheat oven to 400°F. Place 1 tablespoon butter in 9- to 10-inch ovenproof skillet; place skillet in oven to heat while preparing batter. Melt remaining 2 tablespoons butter in small bowl; let cool slightly.

2 Combine flour, granulated sugar and salt in medium bowl; mix well. Add milk, eggs, 2 tablespoons melted butter and vanilla; whisk 1 minute or until batter is very smooth.

3 Remove skillet from oven; immediately pour batter into hot skillet.

4 Bake about 20 minutes or until outside of pancake is puffed and edges are deep golden brown. Sprinkle with powdered sugar; serve with lemon wedges and additional butter.

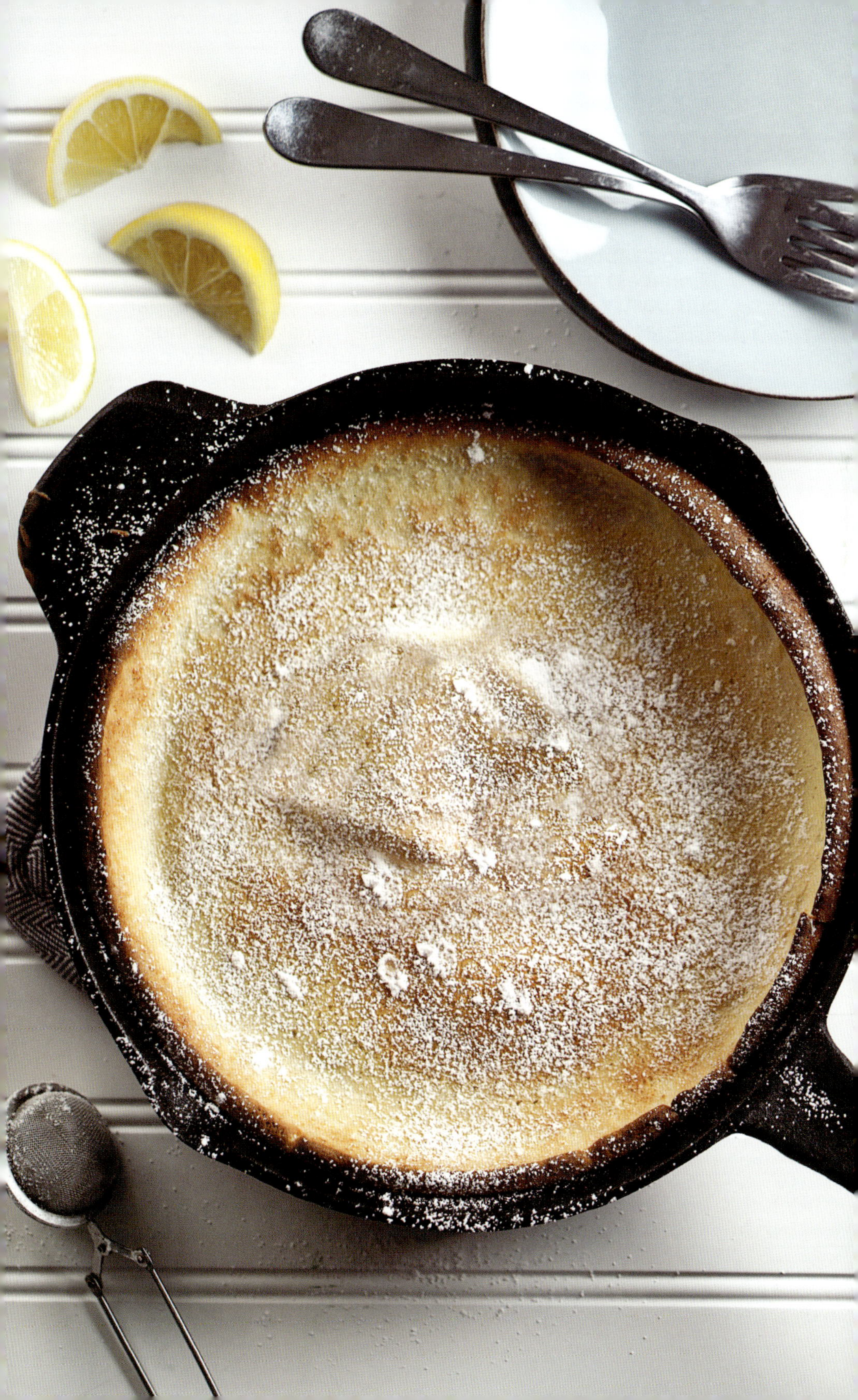

spinach artichoke egg soufflés

makes 8 servings

1 package (about 17 ounces) frozen puff pastry, thawed

1 teaspoon olive oil

¼ cup chopped onion

1 clove garlic, minced

¼ cup finely chopped roasted red pepper (1 pepper)

¼ cup finely chopped canned artichoke hearts (about 2 medium)

¼ cup thawed frozen spinach, squeezed dry

3 eggs, separated

½ (8-ounce) package cream cheese, softened

½ teaspoon salt

⅛ teaspoon black pepper

4 tablespoons grated Romano cheese, divided

1 Preheat oven to 400°F. Spray eight 4-inch or 1-cup ramekins or jumbo (3½-inch) muffin pan cups with nonstick cooking spray. Unfold puff pastry; cut each sheet into quarters. Gently press each pastry square into bottoms and partially up sides of prepared ramekins. (Pastry should not reach tops of ramekins.) Place ramekins on baking sheet; refrigerate while preparing filling.

2 Heat oil in medium skillet over medium heat. Add onion; cook and stir 2 minutes or until softened and lightly browned. Add garlic; cook and stir 30 seconds. Add roasted pepper, artichokes and spinach; cook and stir 2 minutes or until all liquid has evaporated.

3 Whisk egg yolks, cream cheese, salt and black pepper in medium bowl until well blended. Stir in vegetable mixture and 3 tablespoons Romano cheese.

4 Beat egg whites in large bowl with electric mixer at high speed 3 minutes or until stiff peaks form. Fold into vegetable mixture until blended. Divide mixture evenly among pastry-lined ramekins; sprinkle with remaining 1 tablespoon Romano cheese. Fold corners of pastry towards center.

5 Bake 25 minutes or until pastry is golden brown and filling is puffed. Cool in ramekins 2 minutes; remove to wire rack. Serve warm.

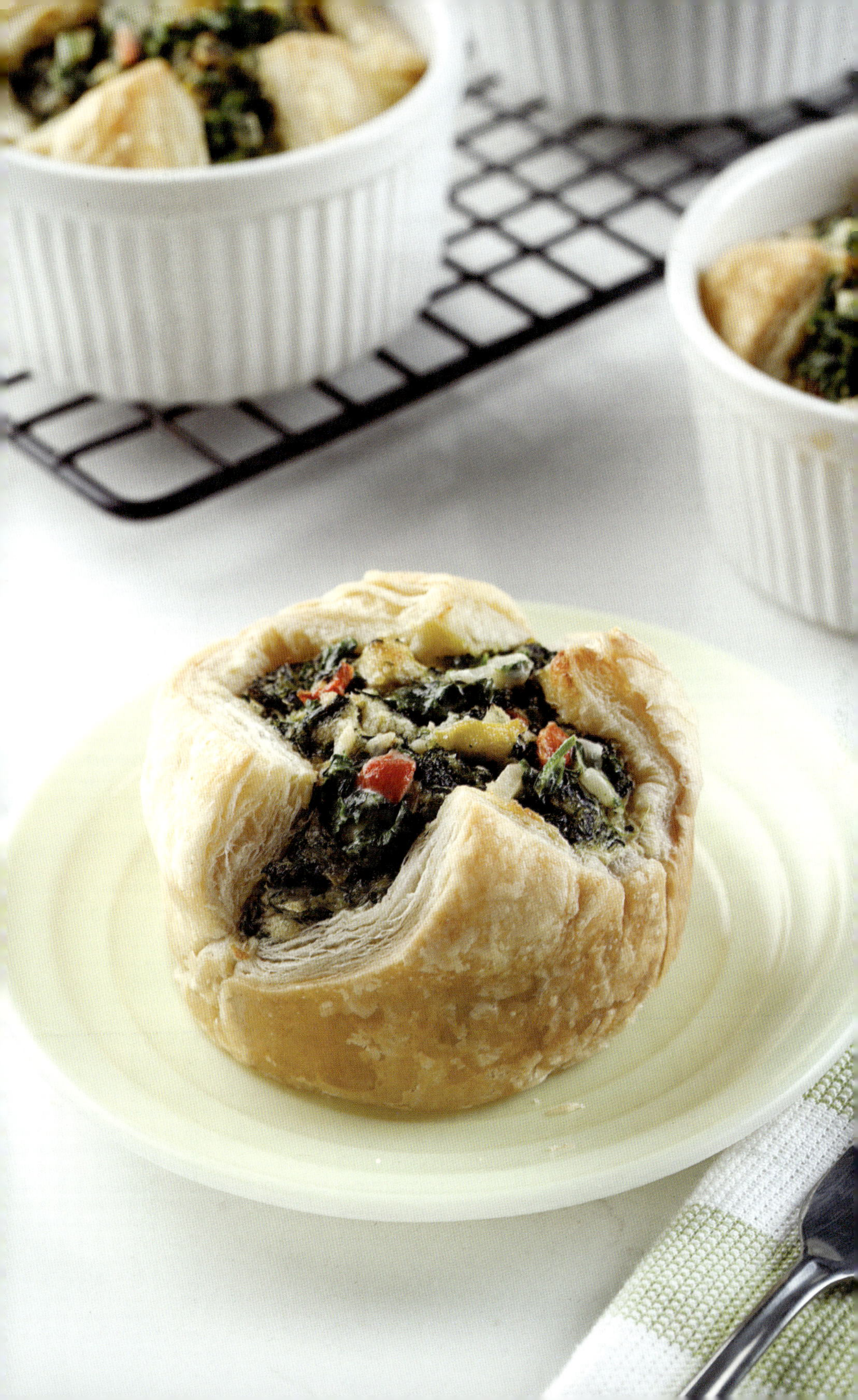

bacon and egg breakfast casserole

makes 6 servings

crust

- 2 cups riced cauliflower (fresh or frozen)
- ½ cup shredded Parmesan cheese
- 1 egg
- ½ teaspoon salt
- ⅛ teaspoon ground red pepper (optional)

filling

- 1 package (12 ounces) bacon, chopped
- 1 onion, chopped
- 1 jalapeño pepper, seeded and chopped
- 2 cloves garlic, minced
- 1 cup (4 ounces) shredded Cheddar cheese, divided
- 8 eggs
- ¾ cup milk
- ¼ teaspoon salt

1 Preheat oven to 400°F. Place cauliflower in medium bowl; cover with plastic wrap and cut slit to vent. Microwave on HIGH 6 minutes. Uncover; cool slightly. Press cauliflower with paper towels to remove excess moisture.

2 Add Parmesan, 1 egg, ½ teaspoon salt and red pepper, if desired; mix well. Press mixture onto bottom and up side of 8-inch square baking dish. Bake 15 minutes. Remove to wire rack. *Reduce oven temperature to 350°F.*

3 Meanwhile, cook bacon in large skillet over medium heat until crisp. Drain on paper towel-lined plate. Drain all but 1 tablespoon drippings from skillet; heat over medium heat. Add onion; cook and stir 5 minutes or until onion is softened. Add jalapeño and garlic; cook and stir 30 seconds. Remove from heat. Spread all but ¼ cup bacon and onion mixture in crust; sprinkle with ¾ cup Cheddar.

4 Whisk eggs, milk and ¼ teaspoon salt in large bowl until well blended. Pour into crust.

5 Bake 30 minutes. Sprinkle with remaining ¼ cup Cheddar and remaining bacon mixture; bake 5 minutes or until cheese is melted.

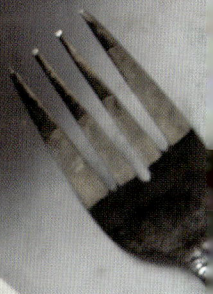

soups, snacks & sides

hot and sour soup

makes 4 servings

2 cans (about 14 ounces each) chicken broth

1 can (4 ounces) sliced mushrooms

2 tablespoons rice vinegar or white wine vinegar

¼ to ½ teaspoon hot pepper sauce

2 tablespoons soy sauce

2 tablespoons cornstarch

1 egg, lightly beaten

2 green onions, thinly sliced, plus additional for garnish

Thinly sliced red bell pepper (optional)

1 Combine broth, mushrooms, vinegar and hot pepper sauce in medium saucepan; bring to a boil over high heat.

2 Stir soy sauce into cornstarch in small bowl until smooth. Add to soup; stir over medium-high heat until slightly thickened.

3 Gradually pour in egg, stirring in one direction 1 minute or until egg is cooked. Remove from heat; stir in 2 green onions. Garnish with additional green onion and bell pepper.

tip

For a heartier soup, add shredded cooked chicken to the broth before thickening it.

yorkshire pudding

makes 6 to 8 servings

1 **cup milk**

2 **eggs**

½ **teaspoon salt**

1 **cup all-purpose flour**

¼ **cup reserved drippings from roast or melted butter**

1 Combine milk, eggs and salt in blender or food processor; blend 15 seconds. Add flour; blend 2 minutes. Let batter stand in blender at room temperature 30 minutes to 1 hour.

2 Preheat oven to 450°F. Place meat drippings in 9-inch square baking pan. Heat in oven 5 minutes.

3 Blend batter 10 seconds; pour into hot drippings. *Do not stir.* Immediately return pan to oven. Bake 20 minutes. *Reduce oven temperature to 350°F;* bake 10 minutes or until pudding is golden brown and puffed. Cut into squares. Serve warm.

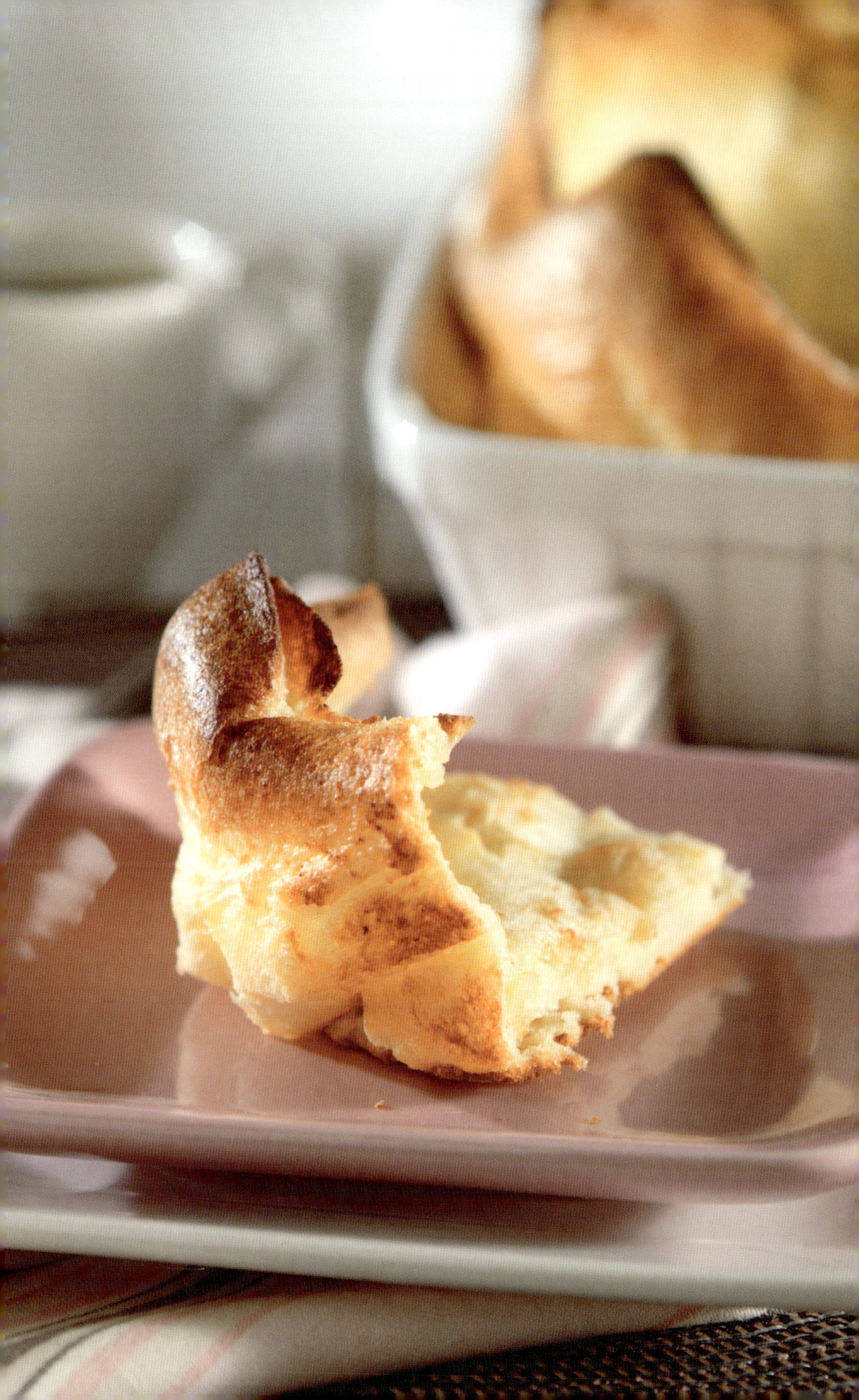

diner egg salad sandwiches

makes 4 servings

6 eggs
2½ tablespoons mayonnaise
1½ tablespoons sweet pickle relish
½ cup finely chopped celery
½ teaspoon salt
Black pepper
8 slices whole grain bread

1 Place eggs in medium saucepan; add cold water to cover. Bring to a boil over high heat. Immediately reduce heat to low; cook 10 minutes.

2 Drain and peel eggs under cold water. Cut eggs in half. Place egg yolks in medium bowl; set aside egg whites.

3 Add mayonnaise and pickle relish to egg yolks; mash with fork until mixture is well blended and creamy.

4 Chop egg whites; add to yolk mixture with celery and salt. Stir gently until blended. Season to taste with pepper.

5 Spread ½ cup egg salad on each of 4 bread slices; top with remaining bread slices. Cut sandwiches in half.

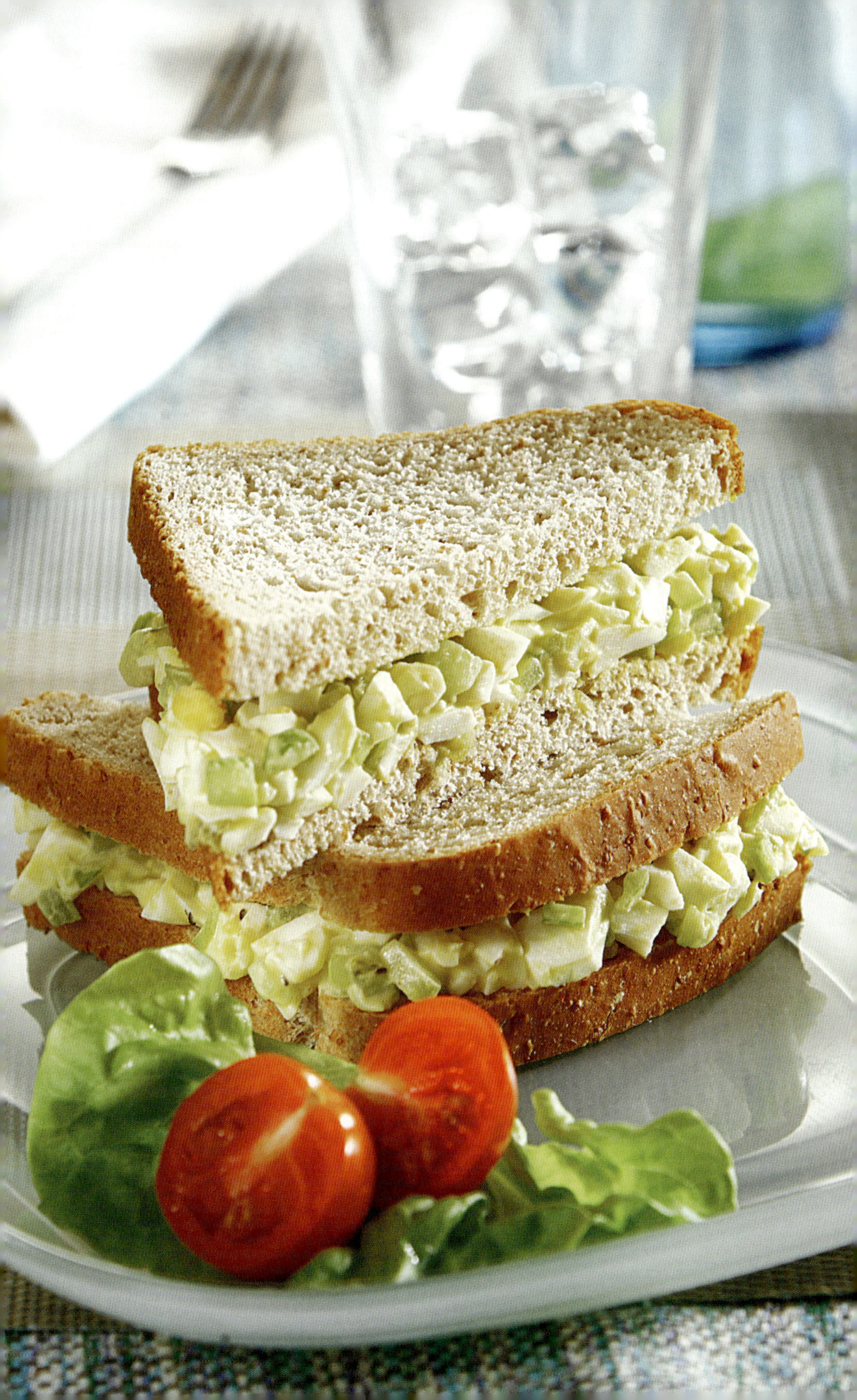

apple-cranberry kugel

makes 6 servings

8 ounces uncooked
  extra-wide egg
  noodles
6 egg yolks
¾ cup sugar
1⅓ cups milk
1⅓ cups whipping cream
1 teaspoon vanilla
¼ teaspoon ground
  cinnamon
⅛ teaspoon salt
2 cups sliced apples
1 cup dried cranberries

1 Preheat oven to 350°F. Spray 8-inch square baking dish with nonstick cooking spray. Cook noodles according to package directions; drain and rinse under cold water.

2 Whisk egg yolks and sugar in medium bowl until thick and pale yellow. Whisk in milk, cream, vanilla, cinnamon and salt until well blended.

3 Combine noodles, apples and cranberries in large bowl; transfer to prepared baking dish. Pour 3 cups egg mixture over noodles. Cover with foil.

4 Bake 55 minutes or just until set. (Center will set as it cools.) Meanwhile, cook and stir remaining egg mixture in small saucepan over low heat 8 minutes or until mixture coats back of spoon. Drizzle over warm kugel.

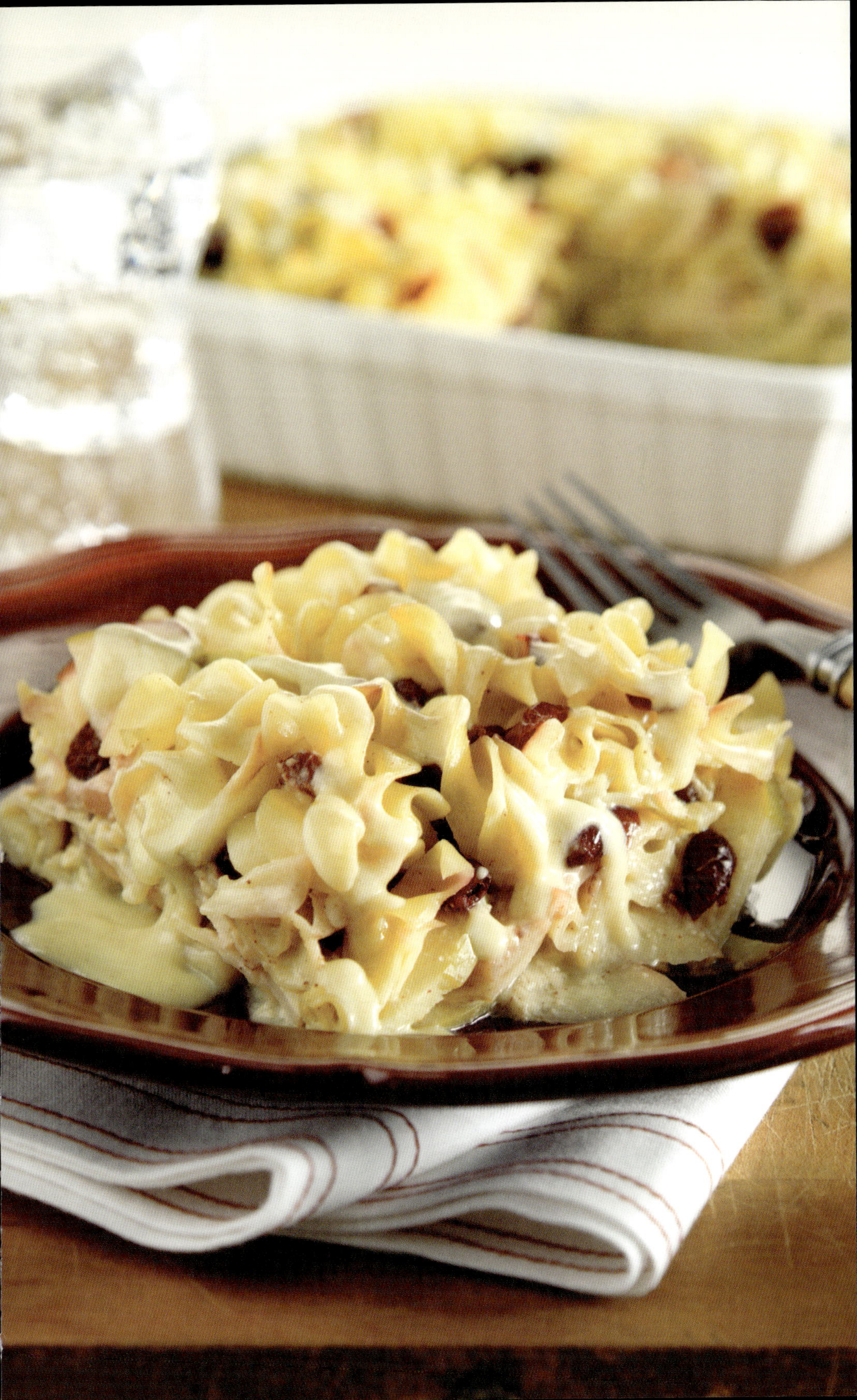

market salad

makes 4 servings

3 eggs

4 cups mixed baby salad greens

2 cups green beans, cut into 1½-inch pieces, cooked and drained

4 slices thick-cut bacon, crisp-cooked and crumbled

1 tablespoon minced fresh basil, chives or Italian parsley

3 tablespoons olive oil

1 tablespoon red wine vinegar

1 teaspoon Dijon mustard

¼ teaspoon salt

¼ teaspoon black pepper

1 Place eggs in small saucepan with enough water to cover; bring to a boil over medium-high heat. Immediately remove from heat; cover and let stand 10 minutes. Drain eggs; cool to room temperature.

2 Combine salad greens, green beans, bacon and basil in large serving bowl. Peel and coarsely chop eggs; add to serving bowl.

3 Whisk oil, vinegar, mustard, salt and pepper in small bowl until well blended. Drizzle dressing over salad; toss gently to coat.

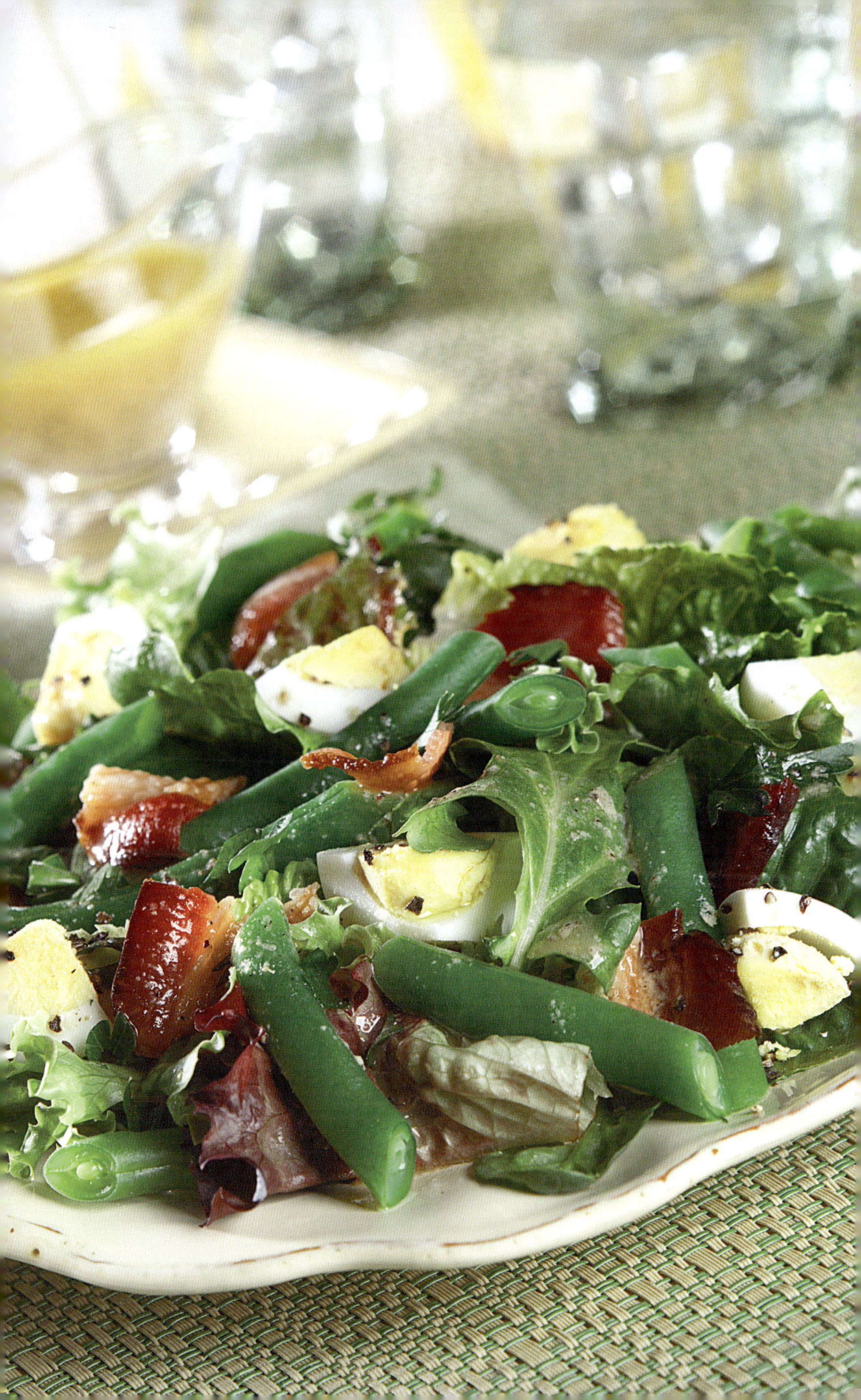

egg drop soup

makes 4 servings

4 cups chicken broth

2 tablespoons
soy sauce

1 tablespoon
dry sherry

1 tablespoon water

1 tablespoon
cornstarch

2 eggs, well beaten

2 green onions,
thinly sliced
on the diagonal

2 teaspoons dark
sesame oil

1 Combine broth, soy sauce and sherry in large saucepan; bring to a boil over high heat. Reduce heat to low; simmer 2 minutes.

2 Stir water into cornstarch in small bowl until smooth. Stir into soup until blended. Cook and stir 3 minutes or until soup is slightly thickened.

3 Stirring constantly in one direction, slowly add eggs to soup in thin, steady stream. Stir in green onions. Remove from heat; stir in sesame oil. Serve immediately.

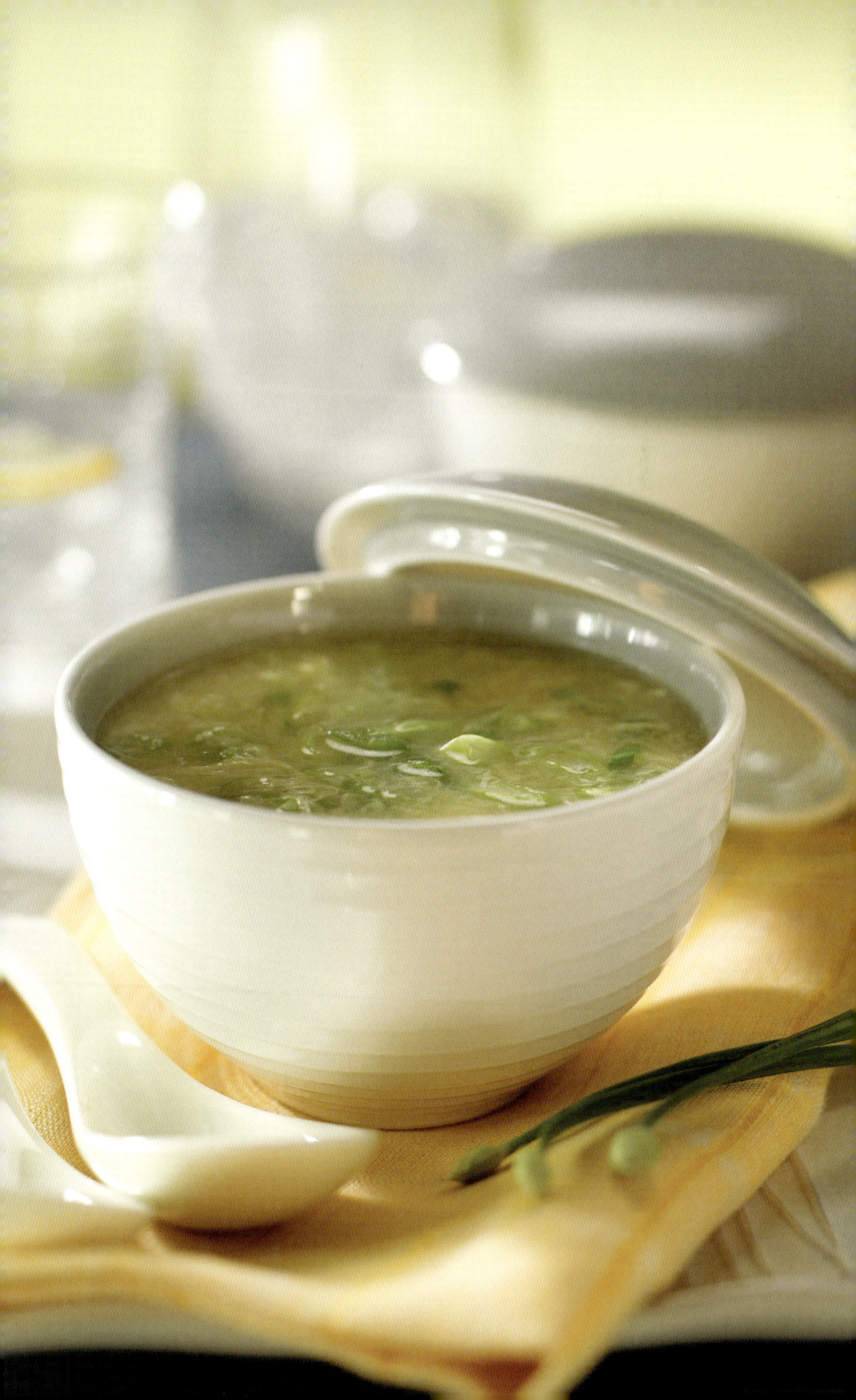

classic deviled eggs

makes 12 deviled eggs

6 eggs

3 tablespoons mayonnaise

½ teaspoon apple cider vinegar

½ teaspoon yellow mustard

⅛ teaspoon salt

Optional toppings: black pepper, minced fresh chives, minced red onion, capers, chopped fresh dill and/or smoked paprika

1 Bring medium saucepan of water to a boil. Gently add eggs with slotted spoon. Reduce heat to maintain a simmer; cook 12 minutes.

2 Meanwhile, fill medium bowl with cold water and ice cubes. Drain eggs and place in ice water; cool 10 minutes.

3 Carefully peel eggs. Cut eggs in half; place yolks in small bowl. Add mayonnaise, vinegar, mustard and salt; mash until well blended.

4 Spoon yolk mixture into egg whites; garnish with desired toppings.

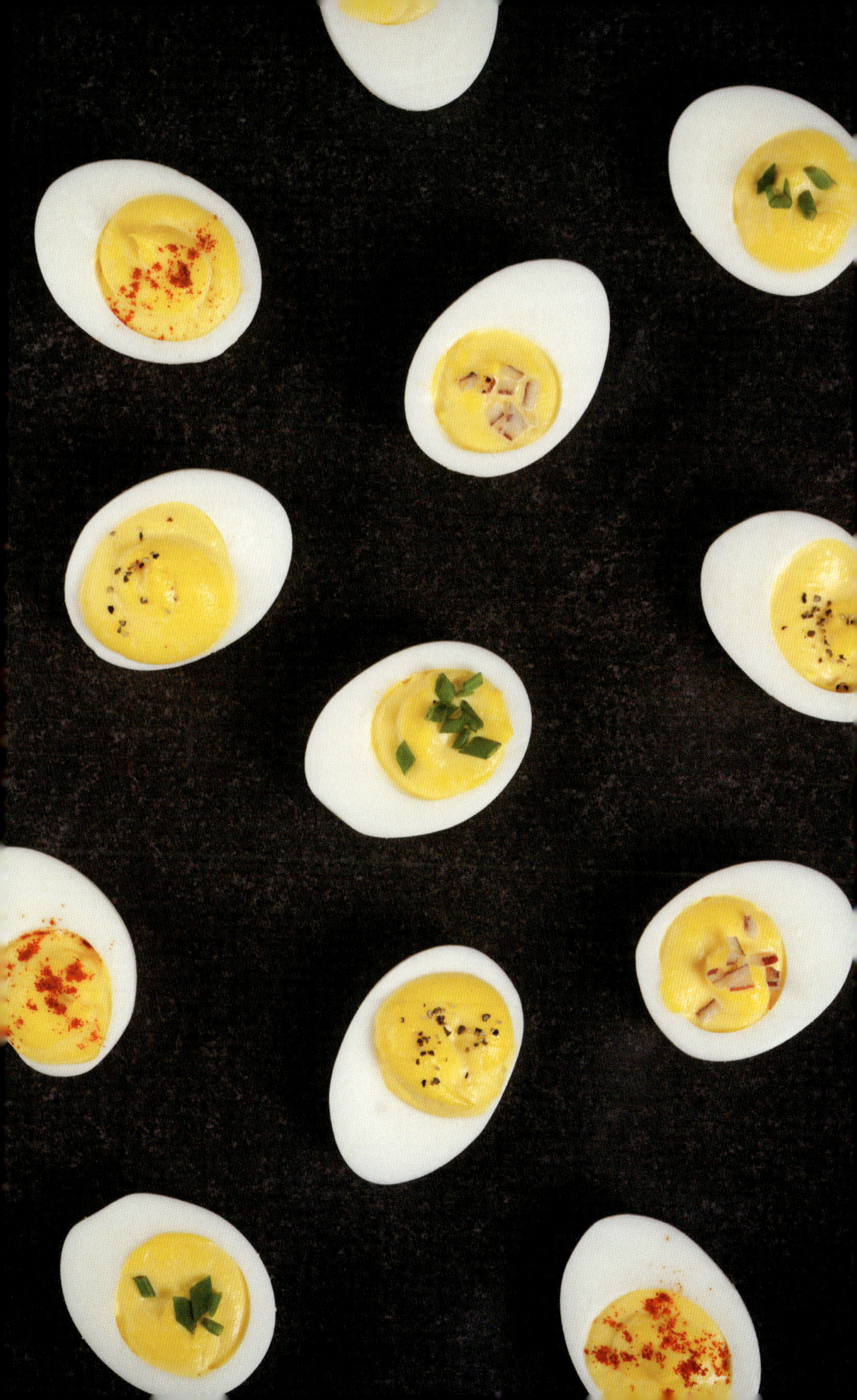

cauliflower picnic salad

makes 6 servings

2 teaspoons salt

1 head cauliflower, cut into 1-inch florets

¾ cup mayonnaise

1 tablespoon yellow mustard

2 tablespoons minced fresh parsley

⅓ cup chopped dill pickle

⅓ cup minced red onion

2 hard-cooked eggs, chopped

Salt and black pepper

1 Fill large saucepan with 1 inch water. Bring to a simmer over medium-high heat; stir in salt and cauliflower. Reduce heat to medium; cover and cook 5 to 7 minutes or until cauliflower is fork-tender but not mushy. Drain and cool slightly.

2 Whisk mayonnaise, mustard and parsley in large bowl until well blended. Stir in pickle and onion.

3 Add cauliflower and eggs; stir gently to coat. Season with salt and pepper.

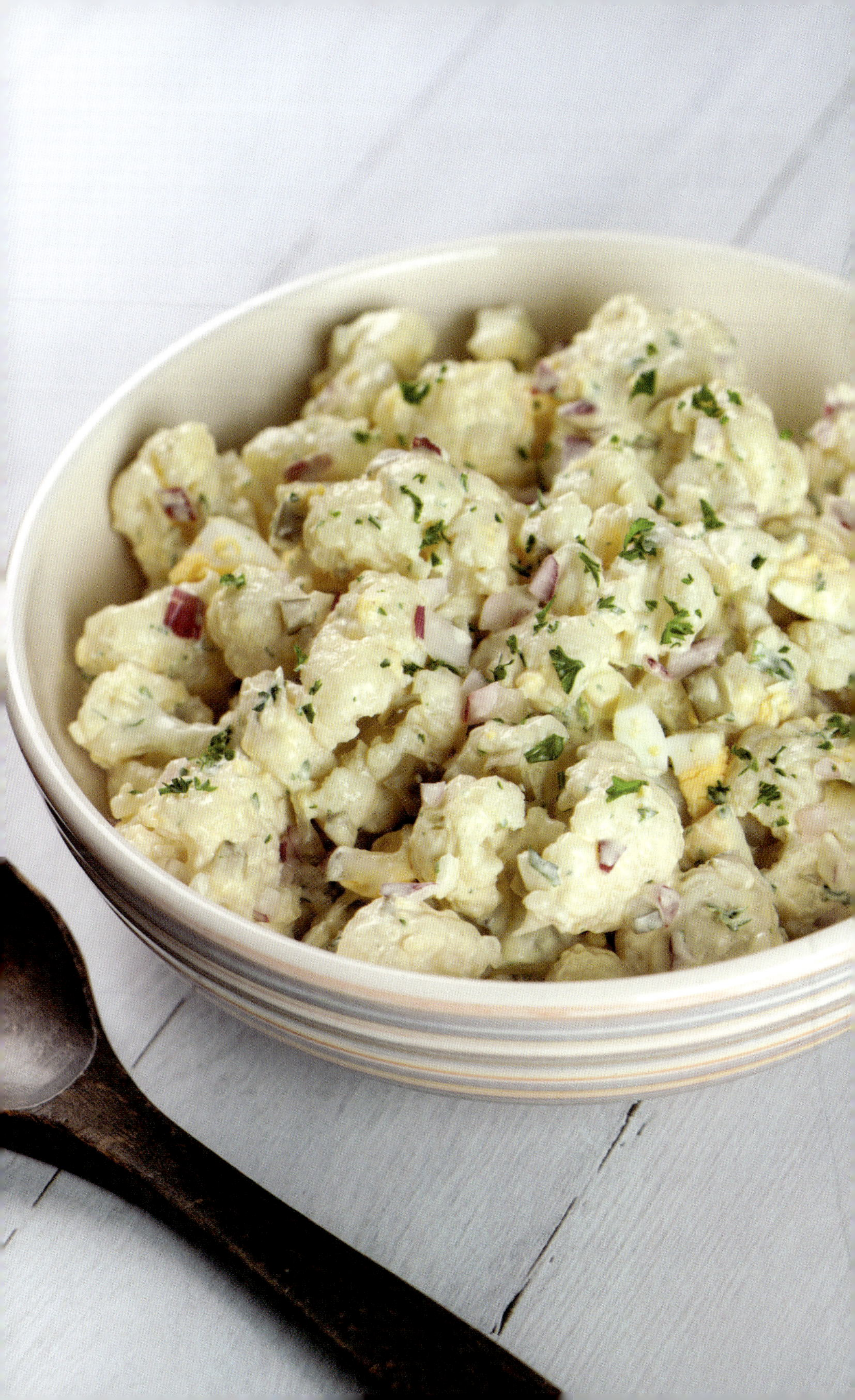

greek lemon and rice soup

makes 6 to 8 servings

2 tablespoons butter

⅓ cup minced green onions

6 cups chicken broth

⅔ cup uncooked long grain rice

4 eggs

Juice of 1 lemon

⅛ teaspoon black pepper (optional)

Fresh mint and lemon peel (optional)

1 Melt butter in medium saucepan over medium heat. Add green onions; cook and stir about 3 minutes or until tender.

2 Stir in broth and rice; bring to a boil over medium-high heat. Reduce heat to low; cover and simmer 20 to 25 minutes or until rice is tender.

3 Beat eggs in medium bowl. Stir in lemon juice and ½ cup broth mixture until blended. Gradually pour egg mixture into broth mixture in saucepan, stirring constantly. Cook and stir over low heat 2 to 3 minutes or until soup thickens enough to lightly coat spoon. *Do not boil.*

4 Stir in pepper, if desired. Garnish with mint and lemon peel.

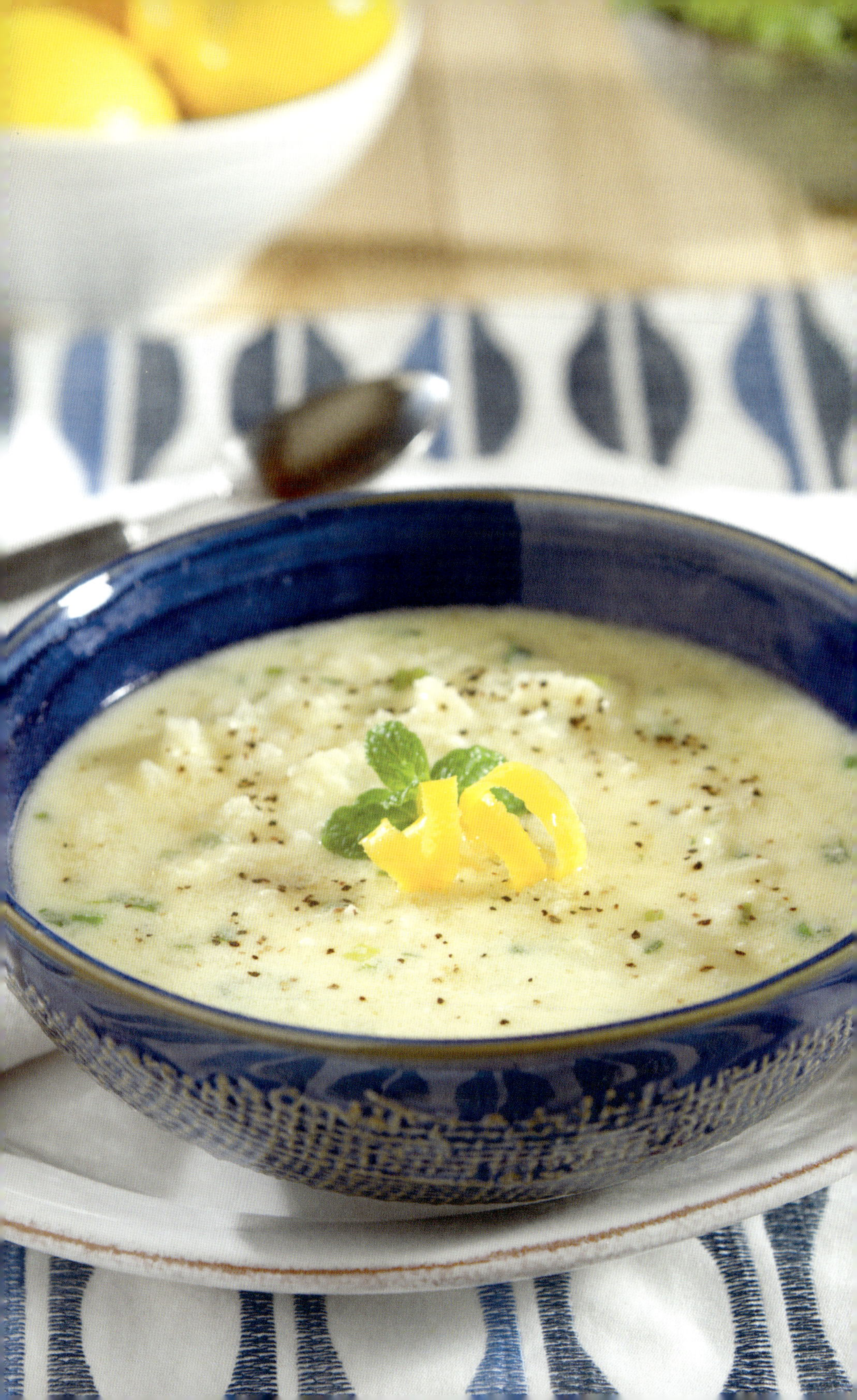

niçoise salad wraps

makes 2 servings

½ cup bite-size green
  bean pieces

2 new red potatoes,
  each cut into
  8 wedges

2 tablespoons
  vinaigrette, divided

1 egg

2 cups watercress
  leaves

4 ounces water-packed
  albacore tuna,
  drained and flaked
  (about ½ cup)

8 niçoise olives, pitted
  and halved

3 cherry tomatoes,
  quartered

2 (10-inch) whole
  wheat tortillas

1 Bring 8 cups water to a boil in large saucepan over high heat. Add green beans and potatoes. Reduce heat to low; cook 6 minutes or until vegetables are tender. Remove vegetables with slotted spoon to bowl of ice water to stop cooking. Drain on paper towels. Transfer to medium bowl; toss with 1 tablespoon vinaigrette.

2 Return water to a boil. Add egg; reduce heat to medium-low and cook 12 minutes. Remove to bowl of ice water to cool; peel and cut into 8 wedges.

3 Add watercress, tuna, olives, tomatoes and remaining 1 tablespoon vinaigrette to vegetables; toss gently to coat.

4 Heat tortillas in nonstick skillet over medium-high heat about 1 minute per side or until softened. Place on plates. Divide salad between tortillas; top with egg wedges. Roll up tortilla to enclose filling. Cut each roll in half before serving.

scotch eggs

makes 8 servings

10 eggs, divided

2 tablespoons vegetable oil

1½ cups panko bread crumbs

1 pound bulk breakfast sausage

¼ cup thinly sliced green onions

¾ cup all-purpose flour

2 tablespoons whole grain mustard

1 Preheat oven to 400°F. Line large baking sheet with foil.

2 Place 8 eggs in large saucepan filled with cold water; cover and bring to a boil over medium-high heat. Turn off heat; let stand 10 minutes. Run eggs under cool water to stop cooking. When cool enough to handle, carefully crack and peel eggs.

3 Meanwhile, heat oil in medium skillet over medium heat. Add panko; cook about 8 minutes or until toasted and golden brown, stirring occasionally. Remove to medium bowl; let cool.

4 Combine sausage and green onions in medium bowl. Place flour in shallow bowl. Lightly beat remaining 2 eggs and mustard in another shallow bowl.

5 Scoop out one eighth of sausage mixture; press flat in palm of your hand. Place 1 cooked egg in center of mixture and wrap sausage around it. Gently roll between your hands until sausage completely encloses egg. Coat sausage-wrapped egg with flour, shaking off excess. Dip in egg-mustard mixture; roll in panko to coat. Place on prepared baking sheet. Repeat with remaining eggs and sausage.

6 Bake 16 to 18 minutes or until sausage is cooked through. Drain well on paper towel-lined plate. Serve immediately.

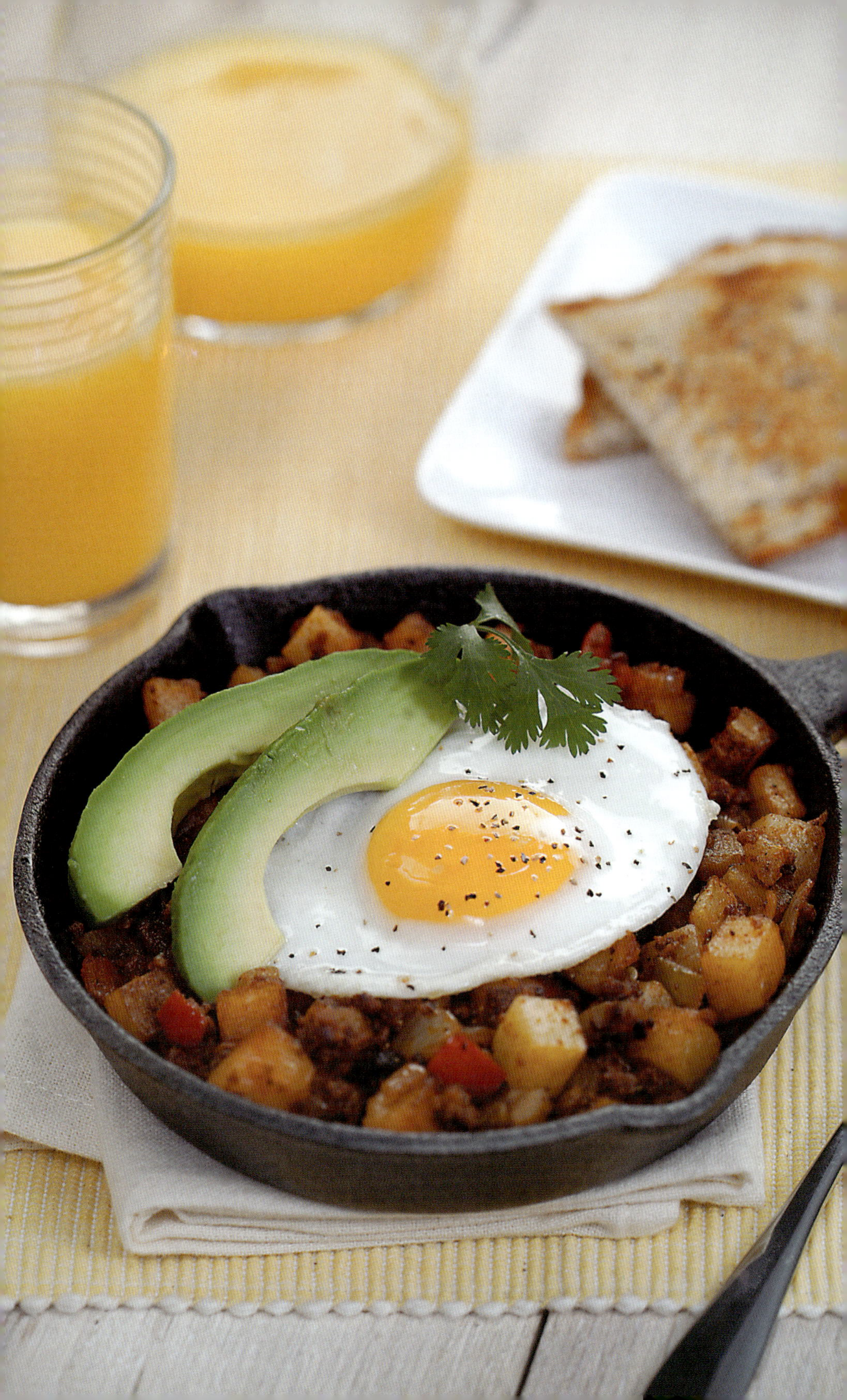

skillet & slow cooker eggs

chorizo hash
makes 4 servings

- 2 unpeeled russet potatoes, cut into ½-inch pieces
- 3 teaspoons salt, divided
- 8 ounces uncooked Mexican chorizo sausage
- 1 yellow onion, chopped
- ½ red bell pepper, chopped (about ½ cup)
- Fried, poached or scrambled eggs
- Avocado slices (optional)
- Fresh cilantro leaves (optional)

1 Fill medium saucepan half full with water. Add potatoes and 2 teaspoons salt; bring to a boil over high heat. Reduce heat to medium-low; cook about 8 minutes. (Potatoes will be firm.) Drain well.

2 Meanwhile, remove and discard casing from chorizo. Crumble chorizo into large skillet; cook and stir over medium-high heat about 5 minutes or until lightly browned. Add onion and bell pepper; cook and stir 4 minutes or until vegetables are softened.

3 Stir in potatoes and remaining 1 teaspoon salt; cook 10 to 15 minutes or until vegetables are tender and potatoes are lightly browned, stirring occasionally. Top with eggs; garnish with avocado and cilantro.

french toast bread pudding

makes 6 to 8 servings

2 tablespoons packed dark brown sugar

2½ teaspoons ground cinnamon

1 loaf (24 ounces) Texas toast-style bread*

2 cups whipping cream

2 cups half-and-half

2 teaspoons vanilla

¼ teaspoon salt

4 egg yolks

1¼ cups granulated sugar

¼ teaspoon ground nutmeg

Maple syrup

Whipped cream (optional)

If unavailable, cut day-old 24-ounce loaf of white sandwich bread into 1-inch-thick slices.

slow cooker directions

1 Spray 3½-quart oval slow cooker with nonstick cooking spray. Combine brown sugar and cinnamon in small bowl. Reserve 1 tablespoon; set aside.

2 Cut bread slices in half diagonally. Using heels on bottom, if desired, arrange bread slices in single layer in bottom of slow cooker, keeping as flat as possible. Sprinkle with rounded tablespoon cinnamon mixture. Repeat layers of bread and cinnamon mixture, keeping layers as flat as possible. Tuck bread into vertical spaces, if necessary.

3 Combine cream, half-and-half, vanilla and salt in large saucepan; bring to a boil over medium heat. Keep warm over low heat.

4 Meanwhile, whisk egg yolks and granulated sugar in medium bowl. Add ¼ cup hot cream mixture, whisking constantly. Add egg mixture to remaining cream mixture in saucepan. Increase heat to medium-high; cook about 5 minutes or until mixture thickens slightly, whisking constantly. *Do not boil.* Remove from heat; stir in nutmeg. Pour mixture over bread and press bread down lightly. Sprinkle with reserved cinnamon mixture.

5 Cover; cook on LOW 3 to 4 hours or on HIGH 1½ to 2 hours or until tester inserted into center comes out clean.

6 Turn off slow cooker. Uncover; let stand 10 minutes before serving with maple syrup and whipped cream, if desired.

pepper and egg couscous bowl

makes 4 servings

1 tablespoon olive oil

3 bell peppers, assorted colors, cut into thin strips

1 red onion, thinly sliced

2 cups vegetable broth

1 cup uncooked instant couscous

1 clove garlic, minced

½ teaspoon salt

½ teaspoon dried oregano

½ teaspoon ground cumin

4 to 8 eggs, fried or poached

1 can (about 15 ounces) black beans, rinsed and drained

1 cup grape tomatoes, halved

Crumbled queso fresco, cotija or feta cheese (optional)

1 Heat oil in large skillet over medium-high heat. Add bell peppers and onion; cook and stir 5 minutes or until vegetables are tender.

2 Bring broth to a boil in small saucepan over medium-high heat. Stir in couscous, garlic, salt, oregano and cumin. Remove from heat; cover and let stand 5 minutes. Fluff with fork.

3 Serve vegetables, eggs and beans over couscous; top with tomatoes and cheese, if desired.

ham and egg breakfast panini

makes 2 sandwiches

1 tablespoon butter

¼ cup chopped green or red bell pepper

2 tablespoons sliced green onion

1 slice (1 ounce) smoked deli ham, chopped

2 eggs

⅛ teaspoon salt

Black pepper

4 slices multigrain or whole grain bread

2 slices Cheddar or Swiss cheese

1 Melt butter in small nonstick skillet over medium heat. Add bell pepper and green onion; cook and stir 4 minutes or until crisp-tender. Stir in ham.

2 Whisk eggs, salt and black pepper in small bowl until well blended. Pour egg mixture into skillet; cook 2 minutes or until egg mixture is almost set, stirring occasionally.

3 Heat grill pan or medium skillet over medium heat. Spray one side of each bread slice with nonstick cooking spray; turn bread over. Top two bread slices with cheese slice, half of egg mixture and remaining bread slices.

4 Grill sandwiches 2 minutes per side, pressing down lightly with spatula until toasted. (Cover pan with lid during last 2 minutes of cooking to melt cheese, if desired.) Serve immediately.

eggs benedict with smoked salmon and hollandaise sauce

makes 4 servings

Hollandaise Sauce
(recipe follows)

1 teaspoon white
   vinegar

8 eggs

4 English muffins,
   split and toasted

4 ounces sliced
   smoked salmon

8 tomato slices

⅓ cup chopped
   fresh dill

1 Prepare Hollandaise Sauce. Keep warm in heatproof bowl set over pan of simmering water, stirring occasionally.

2 Fill large skillet with 2 inches water and vinegar; bring to a simmer over medium heat. Break 4 eggs into four ramekins or small bowls. Holding ramekins close to water's surface, slip eggs into water.

3 Cook eggs about 3 minutes or until whites are completely set and yolks begin to thicken but are not hard. Remove eggs from water with slotted spoon; drain over paper towel. Repeat with remaining eggs.

4 Top each muffin half with salmon, tomato and poached egg. Spoon generous tablespoonful of sauce over each egg; sprinkle with dill. Serve immediately.

hollandaise sauce

makes about 1 cup

3 **egg yolks**
¼ **cup water**
2 **tablespoons lemon juice**
½ **cup (1 stick) cold butter, cut into 8 pieces**
¼ **teaspoon salt**

1 Combine egg yolks, water and lemon juice in small saucepan; gently whisk over very low heat about 4 minutes or until mixture begins to bubble around edges.

2 Whisk in butter, 1 piece at a time, until butter is melted and sauce has thickened. Whisk in salt. Do not allow sauce to boil.

sunny day breakfast burritos

makes 4 servings

1 tablespoon butter

½ cup red or green bell pepper, chopped

2 green onions, sliced

6 eggs

2 tablespoons milk

¼ teaspoon salt

4 (7-inch) flour tortillas, warmed

½ cup (2 ounces) shredded colby jack or Mexican cheese blend

½ cup salsa

1 Melt butter in medium nonstick skillet over medium heat. Add bell pepper and green onions; cook and stir about 3 minutes or until vegetables are softened.

2 Whisk eggs, milk and salt in medium bowl until well blended.

3 Pour egg mixture into skillet. Reduce heat to low; cook until eggs are just set, stirring gently. (Eggs should be soft with no liquid remaining.)

4 Spoon one fourth of egg mixture down center of each tortilla; top with 2 tablespoons cheese. Fold in sides of tortillas to enclose filling. Serve with salsa.

slow-cooked shakshuka

makes 6 servings

1 can (28 ounces) crushed tomatoes with basil, garlic and oregano

1 medium onion, chopped

1 large red bell pepper, chopped

¼ cup extra virgin olive oil

3 cloves garlic, sliced

2 teaspoons sugar

2 teaspoons paprika

2 teaspoons ground cumin

¾ teaspoon salt

¼ teaspoon red pepper flakes

¾ cup crumbled feta cheese

6 eggs

slow cooker directions

1 Combine tomatoes, onion, bell pepper, oil, garlic, sugar, paprika, cumin, salt and red pepper flakes in slow cooker; mix well.

2 Cover; cook on HIGH 3 hours. Stir in feta.

3 Break eggs, one at a time, onto top of tomato mixture, leaving small amount of space between each.

4 Cover; cook on HIGH 15 to 18 minutes or until egg whites are set but yolks are still creamy. Scoop eggs and sauce into each serving dish.

fettuccine alla carbonara

makes 4 servings

12 ounces uncooked fettuccine

4 ounces pancetta or bacon, cut crosswise into ½-inch pieces

3 cloves garlic, cut into halves

¼ cup dry white wine

⅓ cup whipping cream

1 egg

1 egg yolk

⅔ cup grated Parmesan cheese, divided

Dash white pepper

1 Cook fettuccine according to package directions. Drain pasta and return to saucepan; cover to keep warm.

2 Meanwhile, combine pancetta and garlic in large skillet; cook and stir over medium-low heat 4 minutes or until lightly browned. Drain off all but 2 tablespoons drippings from skillet.

3 Add wine to skillet; cook over medium heat 3 minutes or until wine is almost evaporated. Add cream; cook and stir 2 minutes. Remove from heat; discard garlic.

4 Whisk egg and egg yolk in top of double boiler; place over simmering water and adjust heat to maintain simmer. Whisk in ⅓ cup cheese and pepper; cook and stir until thickened.

5 Pour pancetta mixture over fettuccine; toss to coat. Cook over over medium-low heat until heated through. Add egg mixture; toss to coat. Serve with remaining ⅓ cup cheese.

spinach, mushroom, egg and gruyère rollups

makes 4 servings

1 tablespoon plus 4 teaspoons olive oil, divided

1 large shallot, thinly sliced

1 package (5 to 6 ounces) baby spinach

1 clove garlic, minced

½ teaspoon plus ⅛ teaspoon salt, divided

8 ounces cremini mushrooms, thinly sliced

¼ teaspoon black pepper, divided

2 pieces flatbread (9½×11-inches), warmed

⅔ cup shredded Grùyere cheese

6 eggs

2 tablespoons milk

2 teaspoons Dijon mustard

1 Heat 2 teaspoons oil in large nonstick skillet over medium heat. Add shallot; cook and stir 5 minutes or until softened. Add spinach; cook over medium-high heat 2 minutes until wilted. Add garlic and ¼ teaspoon salt; cook 1 minute, stirring frequently. Remove to medium bowl.

2 Heat 1 tablespoon oil in same skillet over medium-high heat. Add mushrooms, ¼ teaspoon salt and ⅛ teaspoon pepper; cook 6 minutes or until browned, stirring occasionally. Add to spinach mixture. Spread half of spinach-mushroom mixture on each flatbread; sprinkle with cheese.

3 Whisk eggs, remaining ⅛ teaspoon salt, ⅛ teaspoon pepper, milk and mustard in large bowl until well blended.

4 Heat remaining 2 teaspoons oil in same skillet over medium-high heat. Add egg mixture; cook about 1 minute or until eggs are set but not dry, stirring frequently.

5 Spread scrambled eggs on flatbreads; roll up. Cut in half diagonally.

corned beef hash

makes 4 servings

2 large russet potatoes, peeled and cut into ½-inch cubes

½ teaspoon salt

¼ teaspoon black pepper

¼ cup (½ stick) butter

1 cup chopped onion

½ pound corned beef, finely chopped

1 tablespoon horseradish

4 eggs

1 Place potatoes in large skillet; add water to cover. Bring to a boil over high heat. Reduce heat to low; cook 6 minutes. (Potatoes will be firm.) Remove potatoes from skillet; drain well. Sprinkle with salt and pepper.

2 Melt butter in same skillet over medium heat. Add onion; cook and stir 5 minutes. Add corned beef, horseradish and potatoes; mix well. Press mixture with spatula to flatten.

3 Reduce heat to low; cook 10 to 15 minutes. Turn hash in large pieces; pat down and cook 10 to 15 minutes or until bottom is well browned.

4 Meanwhile, bring 1 inch of water to a simmer in small saucepan. Break 1 egg into shallow dish; carefully slide into water. Cook 5 minutes or until white is opaque. Remove with slotted spoon to plate; keep warm. Repeat with remaining eggs.

5 Top each serving of hash with 1 egg. Serve immediately.

sweet treats

angel food cake
makes 10 to 12 servings

1¼ cups cake flour, sifted

1⅓ cups plus ½ cup sugar, divided

12 egg whites

1½ teaspoons vanilla

1¼ teaspoons cream of tartar

¼ teaspoon salt

Fresh strawberries (optional)

1 Preheat oven to 350°F. Sift flour and ½ cup sugar into medium bowl.

2 Beat egg whites, vanilla, cream of tartar and salt in large bowl with electric mixer at high speed until soft peaks form. Gradually add remaining 1⅓ cups sugar, beating until stiff peaks form. Gently fold in flour mixture. Pour into *ungreased* 10-inch tube pan.

3 Bake 35 to 40 minutes or until cake springs back when lightly touched.

4 Invert pan; place on top of clean empty bottle. Let cake cool completely in pan upside down. Serve with strawberries, if desired.

cheese blintzes

makes 8 servings (about 16 blintzes)

1¼ cups milk

1 cup all-purpose flour

3 eggs

1 tablespoon cornstarch

½ teaspoon salt

¼ cup (½ stick) butter, melted, divided

1 container (15 ounces) ricotta cheese

2 packages (3 ounces each) cream cheese, softened

3 tablespoons sugar

¼ teaspoon almond extract

Fruit pie filling, fresh fruit or frozen fruit, thawed (optional)

1 Combine milk, flour, eggs, cornstarch and salt in food processor or blender; process just until smooth. Pour into 1-quart glass measure; let stand 30 minutes.

2 Brush medium nonstick skillet lightly with butter; heat over medium heat. Pour about 3 tablespoons batter into skillet, swirling to cover bottom. Cook 1 to 2 minutes or until bottom is browned. Invert crêpe onto large plate. Repeat with remaining batter, brushing skillet with additional melted butter before cooking each crêpe and stacking cooked crêpes browned side up on plate.

3 Beat ricotta cheese, cream cheese, sugar and almond extract in large bowl with electric mixer at medium speed just until blended.

4 Place 2 tablespoons filling in center of unbrowned side of each crêpe. Fold in sides about 1 inch; fold in opposite edges to enclose filling and form rectangular shape.

5 Melt ½ tablespoon butter in large skillet over medium heat. Add blintzes in batches; cook 2 minutes per side or until heated through. Top with fruit, if desired.

classic flan

makes 6 servings

1½ cups sugar, divided
1 tablespoon water
¼ teaspoon ground cinnamon
3 cups whole milk
3 eggs
3 egg yolks
1 teaspoon vanilla

1 Preheat oven to 300°F.

2 Combine 1 cup sugar, water and cinnamon in medium saucepan; cook over medium-high heat without stirring about 10 minutes or until sugar is melted and mixture is deep golden amber in color. Pour into six 6-ounce ramekins, swirling to coat bottoms. Place ramekins in 13×9-inch baking pan.

3 Heat milk in separate medium saucepan over medium heat until bubbles begin to form around edge of pan.

4 Meanwhile, whisk eggs, egg yolks, vanilla and remaining ½ cup sugar in medium bowl until well blended. Whisk in ½ cup hot milk in thin, steady stream. Gradually whisk in remaining milk. Divide milk mixture evenly among ramekins. Carefully add hot water to baking pan until water comes halfway up sides of ramekins. Cover ramekins with waxed paper or parchment paper.

5 Bake 1 hour 15 minutes or until custard is firm and knife inserted into custard comes out clean. Remove ramekins from baking pan to wire rack; cool completely. Cover and refrigerate until cold. Run small knife around edges of ramekins; invert flan onto serving plates.

double chocolate cookies and cream mousse

makes 8 servings

8 ounces semisweet chocolate, chopped

2½ cups chilled whipping cream, divided

4 egg yolks

Pinch salt

1¼ teaspoons vanilla, divided

¼ cup granulated sugar

23 chocolate sandwich cookies, divided

1 tablespoon powdered sugar

1 Melt chocolate in medium saucepan over very low heat, stirring frequently. Remove from heat; stir in ¼ cup cream until well blended.

2 Combine egg yolks and pinch of salt in medium bowl. Whisk about half of chocolate mixture into egg yolks until blended; whisk egg yolk mixture back into chocolate mixture in saucepan. Cook over low heat 2 minutes, whisking constantly. Remove from heat; cool to room temperature.

3 Beat 1¾ cups cream and 1 teaspoon vanilla in large bowl with electric mixer at high speed until soft peaks form. Gradually beat in granulated sugar; continue beating until stiff peaks form. Fold about one fourth of whipped cream into chocolate mixture; fold chocolate mixture into remaining whipped cream until completely combined.

4 Finely chop 2 cookies; fold into mousse. Coarsely chop 2 cookies for topping. Cut remaining 19 cookies into quarters; set aside. Refrigerate mousse 4 hours or overnight.

5 Beat remaining ½ cup cream in medium bowl with electric mixer at high speed 30 seconds or until

thickened. Add powdered sugar and remaining ¼ teaspoon vanilla; beat until stiff peaks form.

6 Spoon ¼ cup mousse into each of eight wide-mouth half-pint jars. Top with ¼ cup quartered cookies and another ¼ cup mousse. Garnish with dollop of sweetened whipped cream and chopped cookies.

pumpkin ice cream

makes 5½ cups

¾ cup canned pumpkin

½ cup packed brown sugar

¼ cup granulated sugar

2 teaspoons ground cinnamon

1 teaspoon ground ginger

¼ teaspoon salt

1½ cups whipping cream

1 cup whole milk

1 tablespoon molasses

4 egg yolks

1 tablespoon cornstarch mixed with 1 tablespoon cold milk

1 Cook pumpkin in medium saucepan over medium heat 5 minutes, stirring frequently. Add brown sugar, granulated sugar, cinnamon, ginger and salt; cook and stir 1 minute. Whisk in cream, milk and molasses over medium-high heat; bring to a boil, stirring frequently. Remove from heat.

2 Whisk egg yolks in small bowl. Slowly whisk in ½ cup hot pumpkin mixture until blended. Slowly whisk egg yolk mixture back into saucepan in thin, steady stream. Cook over medium heat 2 minutes or until mixture is thick enough to coat back of spoon. Add cornstarch mixture; cook and stir 1 minute.

3 Set fine-mesh strainer over medium bowl. Strain pumpkin mixture through strainer into bowl, pressing with spatula to force mixture through. Fill large bowl half full with cold water and ice. Place bowl with pumpkin mixture in ice bath; stir occasionally until mixture is cool.

4 Cover and refrigerate overnight or churn immediately in ice cream maker according to manufacturer's directions. Pack into freezer container and freeze until firm.

decadent coconut macaroons

makes about 3 dozen cookies

1 package (14 ounces) flaked coconut

¾ cup sugar

6 tablespoons all-purpose flour

¼ teaspoon salt

4 egg whites

1 teaspoon vanilla

1 cup (6 ounces) semisweet or bittersweet chocolate chips, melted

1 Preheat oven to 325°F. Line cookie sheets with parchment paper.

2 Combine coconut, sugar, flour and salt in large bowl; mix well. Beat in egg whites and vanilla. Drop batter by tablespoonfuls 2 inches apart onto prepared cookie sheets.

3 Bake 20 minutes or until cookies are set and golden brown. Immediately remove to wire racks to cool completely.

4 Dip tops of cooled cookies in melted chocolate; place on waxed-paper-lined tray or cookie sheet. Let stand at room temperature until chocolate is set. Store in tightly covered container at room temperature up to 1 week.

bread and butter pudding

makes 8 to 10 servings

3 tablespoons butter, softened

1 pound egg bread or firm white bread, sliced

⅔ cup golden raisins

¾ cup sugar, divided

1 teaspoon ground cinnamon

¼ teaspoon ground nutmeg

2 cups half-and-half

2 cups whole milk

6 eggs

1½ teaspoons vanilla

1 Preheat oven to 350°F. Spray 1½-quart or 13×9-inch baking dish with nonstick cooking spray.

2 Lightly butter both sides of bread slices. Cut into 1½-inch pieces. Combine bread and raisins in prepared baking dish. Combine ¼ cup sugar, cinnamon and nutmeg in small bowl; sprinkle over bread mixture and toss to coat.

3 Whisk half-and-half, milk, eggs, remaining ½ cup sugar and vanilla in large bowl until well blended. Pour over bread mixture; let stand 10 minutes.

4 Bake about 1 hour or until pudding is set, puffed and golden brown. Serve warm or at room temperature.

lemon-lime meringue pie

makes 8 servings

1 unbaked deep-dish 9-inch pie crust

4 eggs, separated

¾ cup plus 1 tablespoon sugar, divided

⅛ teaspoon salt

1 tablespoon cornstarch

½ cup whipping cream

3 tablespoons lemon juice

2 teaspoons grated lemon peel

3 tablespoons lime juice

2 teaspoons grated lime peel

2 tablespoons butter, cut into small pieces

1 Preheat oven to 400°F. Prick holes in bottom of crust with fork. Bake 10 minutes or until light brown. Cool completely on wire rack.

2 *Reduce oven temperature to 325°F.* Whisk egg yolks, ½ cup plus 1 tablespoon sugar and salt in medium saucepan until blended. Stir cornstarch into cream in small bowl until smooth. Whisk into egg yolk mixture.

3 Add lemon juice, lemon peel, lime juice and lime peel; cook and stir over medium heat until thickened. Remove from heat; stir in butter until melted. Pour into crust.

4 Beat egg whites in medium bowl with electric mixer at medium speed until frothy. Add remaining ¼ cup sugar, 1 tablespoon at a time, beating at high speed after each addition until stiff and glossy. Gently spread meringue over filling.

5 Bake 20 minutes or until meringue is golden brown. Cool completely on wire rack.

cranberry pound cake

makes 12 servings

1½ cups sugar

1 cup (2 sticks) butter, softened

¼ teaspoon salt

¼ teaspoon ground mace

4 eggs

2 cups cake flour

1 cup chopped fresh or thawed frozen cranberries

1 Preheat oven to 350°F. Grease and flour 9×5-inch loaf pan.

2 Beat sugar, butter, salt and mace in large bowl with electric mixer at medium speed until light and fluffy. Beat in eggs, one at a time, until well blended. Add flour, ½ cup at a time, beating well at low speed after each addition. Fold in cranberries. Spoon batter into prepared pan.

3 Bake 60 to 70 minutes or until toothpick inserted into center comes out clean. Cool in pan on wire rack 5 minutes. Run knife around edges of pan to loosen cake; cool 30 minutes. Remove from pan; cool completely on wire rack.

tip

If fresh or frozen cranberries aren't available, this cake can be made with dried cranberries. Cover 1 cup dried sweetened cranberries with hot water; let stand 10 minutes to soften. Drain well before using; stir into batter as directed in step 2.

individual orange soufflés

makes 6 servings

3 oranges
1½ tablespoons cornstarch
3 tablespoons orange-flavored liqueur
6 egg whites
⅛ teaspoon salt
6 tablespoons granulated sugar
1½ tablespoons sliced almonds (optional)
Powdered sugar (optional)

1 Preheat oven to 450°F. Spray six individual soufflé dishes (8 to 10 ounces each) with nonstick cooking spray. Place dishes in 13×9-inch baking pan or on baking sheet; set aside.

2 Grate enough orange peel to equal 1½ teaspoons. Cut peel and membrane from oranges; section oranges over 1-quart saucepan. Dice oranges; add to saucepan. (There will be 1½ cups juice and pulp.) Stir in cornstarch until smooth. Cook and stir over medium heat until mixture comes to a boil and thickens slightly. Remove from heat; stir in liqueur and reserved orange peel.

3. Beat egg whites and salt in large bowl with electric mixer at high speed until soft peaks form. Gradually beat in granulated sugar, 1 tablespoon at a time, until stiff peaks form. Fold one fourth of egg white mixture into orange mixture with rubber spatula. Fold all of orange mixture into remaining egg white mixture. Spoon into prepared dishes. Sprinkle with almonds, if desired.

4 Bake 12 to 15 minutes or until soufflés are puffed and browned. Sprinkle with powdered sugar, if desired. Serve immediately.

mocha angel food cake with raspberry sauce

makes 10 to 12 servings

cake

- ¾ **cup cake flour**
- ¼ **cup unsweetened cocoa powder (natural or Dutch process)**
- ⅛ **teaspoon salt**
- 1½ **cups sugar, divided**
- 12 **egg whites, at room temperature**
- 1 **teaspoon cream of tartar**
- 2 **teaspoons instant espresso powder dissolved in 2 teaspoons water**
- 1 **teaspoon vanilla**

raspberry sauce

- 1½ **cups fresh raspberries**
- 2 **teaspoons sugar**
- 1 **to 2 teaspoons lemon juice**

1 Place rack in center of oven; preheat to 325°F.

2 Sift cake flour and cocoa into medium bowl. Add salt and ¾ cup sugar; mix well. Beat egg whites in large bowl with electric mixer at medium speed until foamy. Add cream of tartar; beat at medium-high speed until soft peaks form. Gradually add remaining ¾ cup sugar; beat about 5 minutes or until peaks are glossy and firm but not stiff. Stir in espresso mixture and vanilla.

3 Fold flour mixture into egg whites in four parts, mixing well after each addition. Pour batter into *ungreased* 10-inch tube pan; smooth top. Tap pan gently on countertop several times to remove air bubbles.

4 Bake 40 minutes or until toothpick inserted near center of cake comes out clean. Invert pan; place on top of clean empty bottle. Let cake cool completely in pan upside down. Run thin-bladed knife or spatula around outer edge and inside tube before removing from pan.

5 Place raspberries in food processor or blender; process until smooth. Strain raspberries; stir in 2 teaspoons sugar and lemon juice. Serve sauce with cake.

plum bread pudding

makes 6 to 8 servings

6 cups cubed brioche, egg bread or challah (1-inch cubes)

6 large Italian plums, unpeeled

1 tablespoon butter

¾ cup plus 1 tablespoon sugar, divided

6 eggs

2 cups half-and-half

1 cup milk

1 teaspoon vanilla

½ teaspoon salt

½ teaspoon ground cinnamon

Whipping cream or vanilla ice cream (optional)

1 Preheat oven to 400°F. Spray 9-inch square baking dish with nonstick cooking spray.

2 Spread bread cubes in single layer on ungreased baking sheet. Bake 6 to 7 minutes or until lightly toasted, stirring halfway through baking time. *Reduce oven temperature to 325°F.*

3 Pit plums and cut into thin wedges. Melt butter in large skillet. Add plums and 1 tablespoon sugar; cook over high heat 2 minutes or until plums begin to soften. Remove from heat.

4 Whisk eggs, half-and-half, milk, remaining ¾ cup sugar, vanilla, salt and cinnamon in large bowl until well blended. Stir in bread cubes, plums and any juices. Spoon into prepared baking dish.

5 Bake 60 to 65 minutes or until pudding is firm when gently shaken and knife inserted halfway between center and edge comes out clean. Cool 15 minutes. Serve warm with cream, if desired.

raspberry chocolate mousse pie

makes 10 servings

40 chocolate wafer cookies, finely crushed

½ cup (1 stick) butter, melted

½ cup water

7 tablespoons sugar

5 egg yolks

6 ounces semisweet chocolate, melted and cooled slightly

3 tablespoons raspberry-flavored liqueur (optional)

3½ cups whipped topping, thawed

Whipped cream, fresh raspberries and mint leaves (optional)

1 Combine cookie crumbs and butter in medium bowl; mix well. Press onto bottom of 9-inch springform pan.

2 Combine water and sugar in medium saucepan; bring to a boil over medium-high heat. Boil 1 minute.

3 Place egg yolks in large bowl. Gradually whisk in hot sugar mixture. Return egg yolk mixture to saucepan; whisk over low heat 1 to 2 minutes or until mixture is thick and creamy. Remove from heat; pour mixture back into large bowl.

4 Whisk in melted chocolate and liqueur, if desired. Beat mixture until cool. Fold in whipped topping.

5 Pour mixture into prepared crust; freeze until firm. Let pie stand at room temperature 20 minutes before serving. Remove side of pan; garnish as desired.

metric conversion chart

VOLUME MEASUREMENTS (dry)

$1/8$ teaspoon = 0.5 mL
$1/4$ teaspoon = 1 mL
$1/2$ teaspoon = 2 mL
$3/4$ teaspoon = 4 mL
1 teaspoon = 5 mL
1 tablespoon = 15 mL
2 tablespoons = 30 mL
$1/4$ cup = 60 mL
$1/3$ cup = 75 mL
$1/2$ cup = 125 mL
$2/3$ cup = 150 mL
$3/4$ cup = 175 mL
1 cup = 250 mL
2 cups = 1 pint = 500 mL
3 cups = 750 mL
4 cups = 1 quart = 1 L

VOLUME MEASUREMENTS (fluid)

1 fluid ounce (2 tablespoons) = 30 mL
4 fluid ounces ($1/2$ cup) = 125 mL
8 fluid ounces (1 cup) = 250 mL
12 fluid ounces ($1 1/2$ cups) = 375 mL
16 fluid ounces (2 cups) = 500 mL

WEIGHTS (mass)

$1/2$ ounce = 15 g
1 ounce = 30 g
3 ounces = 90 g
4 ounces = 120 g
8 ounces = 225 g
10 ounces = 285 g
12 ounces = 360 g
16 ounces = 1 pound = 450 g

DIMENSIONS

$1/16$ inch = 2 mm
$1/8$ inch = 3 mm
$1/4$ inch = 6 mm
$1/2$ inch = 1.5 cm
$3/4$ inch = 2 cm
1 inch = 2.5 cm

OVEN TEMPERATURES

250°F = 120°C
275°F = 140°C
300°F = 150°C
325°F = 160°C
350°F = 180°C
375°F = 190°C
400°F = 200°C
425°F = 220°C
450°F = 230°C

BAKING PAN SIZES

Utensil	Size in Inches/Quarts	Metric Volume	Size in Centimeters
Baking or Cake Pan (square or rectangular)	$8 \times 8 \times 2$	2 L	$20 \times 20 \times 5$
	$9 \times 9 \times 2$	2.5 L	$23 \times 23 \times 5$
	$12 \times 8 \times 2$	3 L	$30 \times 20 \times 5$
	$13 \times 9 \times 2$	3.5 L	$33 \times 23 \times 5$
Loaf Pan	$8 \times 4 \times 3$	1.5 L	$20 \times 10 \times 7$
	$9 \times 5 \times 3$	2 L	$23 \times 13 \times 7$
Round Layer Cake Pan	$8 \times 1 1/2$	1.2 L	20×4
	$9 \times 1 1/2$	1.5 L	23×4
Pie Plate	$8 \times 1 1/4$	750 mL	20×3
	$9 \times 1 1/4$	1 L	23×3
Baking Dish or Casserole	1 quart	1 L	—
	$1 1/2$ quart	1.5 L	—
	2 quart	2 L	—